Tactics of Everyday Leadership: Becoming a Plus-One Leader

David B. Whitlark, PhD
Gary K. Rhoads, PhD

BYU ACADEMIC PUBLISHING

Tactics of Everyday Leadership
Becoming a Plus-One Leader:

David B. Whitlark, PhD • Gary K. Rhoads, PhD

Managing Editor
Jennifer Berry

Illustrations
Chris Henderson, Chris Hallstrom, Kent Minson

Cartoons
Donovan Horsechester

Cover Design
Doug Cole

Printer
BYU Print & Mail Production Center

    HARDBACK ISBN: 0-7409-3041-9
    TRADE PAPER ISBN: 0-8425-2640-4

For more information or permission to use material from this text or product contact:
BYU Academic Publishing
3993 WSC
Provo, UT 84602
Tel (801) 422–6231
Fax (801) 422–0070
academicpublishing@byu.edu

To report ideas or text corrections email us at:
textideas@byu.edu

CONTENTS

One of our colleagues at the university mentioned that he once learned in a sociology class that there are three different reasons for people becoming leaders—some people lead because they are charismatic, some people lead because they are experts in their field, and some people lead because they are appointed. This book is written for people who find themselves in situations two and three.

Leadership is one of those topics about which people have lots of questions. If you are one of those people with questions, we've got answers. Are leaders born or made? Yes and yes. Can leadership skills be taught? Yes, but we suppose it depends on how interested you are in learning. Is leadership different than management? No. With all due respect to Peter Drucker, if you are a stumblebum leader, you won't be much of a manager either.

What are the most important talents or skills that a leader can have? Survival skills. Do you give people what they want or what is best for them? Yes and yes. Can a good leader really change things for the better? Yes. What is leadership? To answer that question we'll defer to a surprising and brilliant quote from Ralph Nader. "The function of leadership is to produce more leaders, not more followers."

With *Tactics of Everyday Leadership* we set out to write a fun and entertaining book that builds on our unique (some would say quirky) sense of humor. Some books appear to be written as a medication-free sleeping pill, but not this book! We want the reader to stay awake and alert through the whole ride. Sometimes, however, we get serious for a few particularly important topics. The following discussion of everyday leadership is one of those times.

What is everyday leadership? It is the type of leadership we all need in our everyday lives, whether at work, at home, or at play. It is the type of leadership that we can use day in and day out and still look at ourselves in the mirror and sleep peacefully at night. It is not the grandiose leadership we see so often from political leaders and industry titans. It is simple, humble, and follows the golden rule (and not the golden rule that says, "He who has the gold makes the rules"). It is patient and persuasive. It is not pushy, intimidating or manipulative. One might say everyday leadership is ethical leadership.

Herb Rubenstein, CEO of Growth Strategies, Inc., defines ethical leadership as "the creation and fulfillment of worthwhile opportunities by honorable means." According to his definition, being an ethical leader requires more than being honest. It is being honorable, humane, and high-principled. It is taking the moral high ground. It means not doing things that we know to be wrong. What is unethical leadership? It is accomplishing whatever we want by doing whatever it takes even if we know or simply feel it is wrong. It is frightening to think that unethical leadership potentially creates an action-reaction culture of mind-bending manipulation accompanied by crippling deceit and runaway resentment

Remember the Ralph Nader quote? Leadership is primarily about producing leaders and not followers. Richard Field, a Professor of Strategic Management at the University of Alberta, points out that unethical leadership is primarily concerned with just the opposite. Its goal is to produce obedient, dependent, and compliant followers. It is authoritarian with all the strings being pulled from the top. Plus-One leadership builds from the bottom up, tapping into the dreams, goals, and insights of the rank and file.

Okay, now that we've gotten the serious discussion out of the way, let's get back to the fun. This book instructs the reader on how to become a Plus-One leader. Other than just being a catchy name, "Plus-One leader" carries a special meaning for us. Plus-One leaders have that one extra dimension that elevates them from good to great. Plus-One leaders have the courage to lead and not control. They have the skills to act and not react. They value others at least as much as they value themselves. To be a Plus-One leader you will plan before you act, learn before you plan, and when things take an unexpected negative turn, you will step back, and learn more before letting one false word or cross-eyed look spoil your chances for success!

Becoming a Plus-One Leader is not a book that discusses the latest theory, trend, or leadership fad. It is a book of down-to-earth tactics and practical exercises. From what we have seen, it is easy for even well-meaning leaders to become preoccupied with what they want to do, but give little thought to how to do what they want and how what they say or do may inspire or adversely affect others. In this book we show leaders-in-training how to do what they want and to do it with fairness, flash, and finesse. We take you each step of the way from the behavior of the commonly-seen leader to becoming one who is truly exceptional. As you read through the book, learn the tactics, and master the principles, we believe you will enjoy your transformation as much as we enjoyed our own!

Acknowledgements

Writing even a short a book is a long process and for us the process has taken longer than we want to admit. While writing, we benefited enormously from the help of colleagues, clients, mentors, and students. In particular, we express sincere gratitude to the students in our leadership course as well as our other courses. They have been incredibly generous with their time and energy, giving us the rare opportunity to test and refine our ideas and discover how best to communicate them.

We genuinely appreciate the opportunity we were given to present some of our early ideas for this book at the Marriott School Management Conference. Norm Nemrow and Idon Openshaw took a particularly large leap of faith including us on the program. We want to thank Roger McCarty for helping on an early draft and Jennifer Berry of BYU Academic Publishing for her tremendously dedicated and talented work as our editor and student.

We also are indebted to our beautiful wives and extraordinary families for their patience as we tried out each tactic on them, their inspiration as our motivation for the project waned, and their critical eyes in helping us improve and continue to dream.

David Whitlark
Gary Rhoads

Part ONE

Surviving Leadership

How to Survive as a Leader

Once upon a time there was an employee who very much wanted to be a supervisor. The employee worked hard every day and sacrificed much time and effort to his company. After what seemed to be forever, he was finally promoted. He was excited and vowed to be a better manager than the supervisors for whom he had worked. He eagerly began managing his first employee, politely asking the employee to do a particular task. The employee tried hard, but didn't do the work as efficiently or effectively as the new supervisor wanted.

The new supervisor, following the examples of his previous supervisors, asked again, but this time with a louder voice and not nearly so politely. The employee knew her supervisor was upset, and this stressed her. So she tried much harder to accomplish the task. This time she did a better job and resolved that in the future she would do it right the first time. The supervisor resolved that in the future he wouldn't bother to ask politely. When he wanted something done he just shouted loudly. The employee was OK with that. She realized she needed to be stressed to do her best work. From that day on, the business flourished and the supervisor and the employee worked together happily ever after.

Does this sound like a fairy tale? In today's world it certainly is. But still, at home and at work, we have found ourselves and observed others applying personal pressure rather than using effective leadership skills. The "personal pressure" style of leadership illustrated above has been shown, time after time, to create more resentment than positive results. This leadership style is one of the hallmarks of an individual with no natural leadership ability. And we may as well admit this fact early, so there will be no misunderstanding:

Most of us do not have natural leadership skills.

There of course are people out there, men and women of all ages and backgrounds, in business, in education, civics, and families, etc., who are natural-born leaders. But these are the very, very few. We have researched and written this book for us, not them.

The times, they are a-changin'

Throughout history, there have been individuals with no natural leadership skills, who, either by chance, birth, opportunity or some other quirk of fate, led others, often changing history for good or evil. The people they led might constitute an entire nation, or a huge industry, or a classroom, small workshop, or family unit, but the lack of leadership skills at any level has almost always been identified by the way poor leaders resort to high-pressure tactics, such as shouting, intimidation, threats, humiliation, playing favorites, setting of double standards, and other ways to attempt to meet their goals. History continues, and so does much of the world's leadership, seemingly just by default, rather than merit. Often, most of the people these non-leaders led, whether they were employees, citizens, or family members, just silently accepted all the posturing and ineffective leadership.

Ironically, in today's fast-paced world, where more and more people with no natural leadership ability are expected to exercise solid leadership muscles, the rising generations of followers and workers expect and even frequently demand more effectiveness and better results from their leaders[1]. Truly effective, efficient leaders are needed today more than ever before, and every one of those leaders needs leadership skills that very, very few possess naturally. Our studies have shown that, fortunately, almost everyone can acquire outstand-

---

1.   *Millenials Rising* by Neil Howe and William Strauss

"But Beppy, you can't leave our team now. We built this business together."

© BYU Academic Publishing

ing leadership skills and become the type of effective leader that employees, family, and others love to work for, live with, and just be around.

Another current trend in the employment setting is a shift in the loyalties of the average employee. Gone are the days when employers could expect 30 continuous years of dutiful service from every employee. Instead, the work force has become a mobile set, frequently switching jobs with the promise of better and better opportunities and greater personal reward.

In this world, few, if any employees work only for the pleasure of doing a good job for the company or to make their supervisors look good. Employee loyalty has largely been replaced by a feeling of job entitlement. That is, employees will do a great job, but often only if there are clear benefits to them for doing so. Without these benefits, an employee might quickly jump ship for employment that seems to offer the personal rewards they feel entitled to. Now, more than ever before, employees must be sold on why they should perform well for you and not the business next door. To succeed in this environment, you, as an effective-leader-in-training, must quickly develop your ability to motivate and train others to be successful. In the end, helping your employees find and enjoy the personal rewards of a job well done is mutually beneficial since it will also make it easier for you to retain quality people.

I must survive

Before you can thrive as a leader, you must first learn to recognize and survive the problems inherent in leadership. It has been our experience that when managers are confronted with stressful employee situations, they often become defensive. They put their personal guard up and try to play the role of the expert, the person who has all the answers, regardless of the sometimes obvious fact that they have no answers. Unfortunately, such behavior can easily send this type of leader into an effectiveness tailspin, a downward leadership death spiral. We will discuss this issue in more detail in a moment, but now consider the example of Greg and Denise.

Greg had thirty years experience in the advertising industry when he was hired to head a small publishing company. When Greg arrived to take on his new responsibilities, he met Denise, the publishing company's customer service and publicity manager. She has been with the publishing company for many years and is *the* key player in getting things done. One day Greg read about an emerging news story that linked nicely to a book just published by the company. He saw a small window of opportunity to build awareness for the book if Denise could quickly send out an email blast to national media outlets while simultaneously sending out review copies.

Sensing that Denise was not entirely behind his strategy, in a team meeting Greg demanded that she hire a temp to get the publicity work done for the book. Denise was understandably defensive, saying that a temp couldn't do the job in a professional manner. She was quickly contradicted by another staff member and ultimately left the meeting early, feeling hurt and humiliated.

That situation was never clearly resolved. Now Denise routinely points out problems with Greg's suggestions at staff meetings and Greg backs down each time that Denise pushes back. Everyone on the staff knows that Denise is more important than Greg to the day-to-day operations. Greg realizes he has lost control and can't do a thing about it.

Greg is like many people who take on leadership responsibilities and sincerely think they are doing the right thing for their organization by being "forceful," but instead discover—without having any solution—that their weak or insensitive attitudes just lead to more mistakes and limit their leadership effectiveness. Greg is caught in a leadership death spiral.

All too often we observe potentially great leaders backing into, stumbling into, or marching triumphantly into a leadership death spiral. It is painful to watch because we know those leaders are trying their best and we know that their Herculean efforts to avoid that spiral, or to escape from it once they realize they're in it, will do much more harm than good. This is what makes observing the phenomenon so compelling, seeing leaders spiraling downward who actually think that by building up their defenses or climbing on a higher pedestal they will be escaping from their predicament when they really are just spinning downward faster.

Here is how it works. A manager gets feedback from his supervisor or his employees that he is a weak manager. Of course the manager is concerned and redoubles his efforts to be friendly to every employee, to provide quick and detailed feedback on employee performance, and become more expert on the products, services, or processes he is managing. Every day he tries a little harder. Every day the employees push back a little harder. Finally, the manager takes a stand to protect his authority, he climbs on a pedestal, gets defensive, and may even put in place stricter work rules, a public confrontation follows, and his ability to lead crumbles on the spot.

Managers and employees view this kind of experience very differently. From the manager's point of view, he has done everything possible to be thoughtful and effective. From the employees' perspective, the view is not as positive. Often, they see the manager as just another flattering backslapper who tries too hard, who feels nervous about his job and doesn't have the knowledge or ability to know what should or shouldn't be done.

Leaders, just like followers, all make mistakes. However, there are certain proven leadership skills (many of which are somehow apparently known instinctively by natural-born leaders) that can minimize our leadership mistakes if they are understood and followed. We must first learn to avoid high-pressure leadership tactics and the leadership death spiral to survive as a leader long enough to give us a real chance to thrive as a leader. Over the next chapters, we will introduce basic concepts, laws, and tactics, that form the foundation for what we call Plus-One leadership.

Plus-One leadership

In marketing, we sometimes talk about Plus-One positioning, i.e., positioning a product in the marketplace so that it has all the standard features *plus one* additional feature that sets it apart from other products. This simple idea gave us some thoughts about leadership. In a Plus-One leader we would like to see someone who has all the standard features plus one additional feature that sets him or her apart from other leaders. From what we have read and heard, a lot of people think that one additional feature is charisma.

Can charisma be taught? There are so many people in leadership positions that don't seem to have a drop of it! But we are optimists, and believe, at the very least, that most anyone can learn to significantly elevate whatever natural level of charisma they happen to have. That is the premise of Plus-One leadership. It aims to give leaders at least a small dose of that one additional feature, charisma, to set them apart from other leaders.

Years ago, we took it as a challenge to identify a set of principles and associated tactics that could make even the smelliest old dog well-liked and influential. In other words we were looking for tactics that were simple and powerful enough so that they could help even us. We began the work by making a study of the word charisma.

Charisma is a fascinating word which is related to a Greek word meaning divine gift. In Christianity, it is defined as an extraordinary gift to perform miracles. Worldly definitions revolve around personal magnetism, charm, or special warmth of personality. Certainly, if we look at charisma in terms of leadership, it is a gift that can perform miracles. Also, we see in it special warmth of personality. In fact a respelling of charisma to "caressme" may be in order. Caress means to hold dear. In our way of thinking, caressme is a promise from all people that if their leaders will hold them dear, then in return they will work miracles.

Plus-One leaders can have all those positive characteristics that commonly-seen leaders have plus some extra skills, personal control, confidence, friends, success, and personal satisfaction. There is no downside to becoming a Plus-One leader, only upside potential.

Why we're writing about leadership

By vocation, we research and write about advertising, selling, and sales management. Aside from being academics, on a professional level we've immersed ourselves in the day-to-day work of influencing national audiences via multimillion dollar advertising campaigns as well as influencing individuals via one-to-one personal selling. We know something about the tactics of influence and persuasion. We see the world through tactical eyes.

We listen with interest as the experts talk about leadership. We are eager to learn. But what we hear usually disappoints because it doesn't tell us what we need to do to be an effective leader, to be influential. Recently we heard a speech from a celebrated business leader. We enjoyed the messages, "leaders must lead," "leaders focus," "leaders set high standards," and so on, but we wanted more. We wanted the "how to."

Leaders must influence or they are just leaders "in name only." Yes, organizations do seem to move forward with their own momentum when headed up by such leaders, but one can only wonder what could be accomplished if the leader exercised some tactical leadership skills. We've found having a toolkit of tactics handy for influencing others. Several years ago we started making presentations describing the toolkit to business audiences. Frankly, we were shocked by the positive response. It seems as though most everyone wants the "how to." So we've continued our research. We interview managers, we ask them to experiment with tactics, we ask them to keep leadership journals, and we compile the results—good and bad.

For you, the reader, is recorded the various bits and pieces of what we have uncovered and learned about the tactics of influence over more than twenty years of research and experimentation. We stress exercises and tactics that will make you influential—whether you are the "appointed leader" or simply choose to take on a bigger leadership role within your organization.

Chapter ONE

THE THREE IMMUTABLE LAWS OF SELF-PRESERVATION

The strongest human instinct is to impart information, the second strongest is to resist it.

Kenneth Grahame

L eadership, even when bestowed on truly gifted individuals, is not easy, even though some leaders may make it look effortless. There are lots of barriers and pitfalls from the beginning right up to the close of a leader's career. There are employees who react to a leader's kindness with suspicion, to enthusiasm with opposition, and to true expertise with nitpicking criticism. To survive leadership and avoid the leadership death spiral, the leader-in-training needs to know who and what to look out for and how to get people to push themselves. All of which brings us face-to-face with the three immutable laws of self-preservation.

At the close of the Second World War, which pitted several powerful leaders against each other, our country was concerned about the possibility that some new tyrant would arise who could bend the world's population to his will through the use of the newly emerging mass media[2]. Several studies conducted in late 1940s explored the

---

2.   *Some Principles of Mass Persuasion* by Dorwin Cartwright

power of mass media to influence people. These studies resulted in sociologists postulating over a dozen principles from which we have formulated three laws regarding the use of persuasion on groups. The laws are powerful and useful. Applied to leadership, these laws will help us see how many successful leaders move individuals, groups, and even entire nations to take action.

Law #1: Not everyone loves you

A common leadership mistake when working with people is assuming that everyone wants to hear what we have to say. We ignore the first immutable law. Most of us talk to others as if everyone in the group is sitting on the edge of their seat hanging on to our every word and worshiping what we have to say. As hard as it may be for us to believe, this assumption is rarely true. Studies suggest that in any given audience about twenty percent of the people love you, about twenty percent of the people hate you, and about sixty percent of the people feel indifferent or neutral.

Leadership, like life, is full of diversity. We must recognize that all groups will include people with assorted attitudes towards the subject or conditions that brought the group together. Fortunately, we can learn to connect to this diverse audience if we recognize and successfully relate to its three smaller subgroups—the "love group," "hate group," and "swing group."

Every Group Consists of Three Smaller Groups

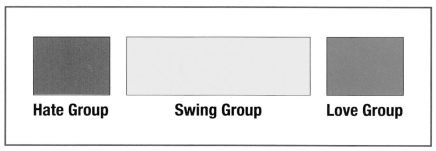

Hate Group   Swing Group   Love Group

Traffic Lights and Groups

A group of people is like a traffic light. There are people that say stop, some that say go, and some that say proceed with caution!

If we address a group with the assumption that everyone loves us, and forget about the reality that most do not, we can expect that only the people who love us even before we speak will still love us after we are done. We must think carefully about what we are doing, how we're doing it, and how others perceive our efforts, or we won't see any positive, much less dramatic change, in attitudes.

An even riskier approach than assuming everyone loves us is to take on the Hate Group. Although it is a natural tendency to assume everyone loves us, sometimes the existence of the Hate Group is painfully obvious. Often, our reaction when confronted by the Hate Group is to take them on directly. However, the ones who hate us before we speak are not likely to put down their torches and pitchforks after we are done and thank us for coming. Even worse, quite likely the things we do as leaders will cause this group to hate us even more. Additionally, by aiming our best persuasive efforts at the most negative and vocal elements of an audience, everyone may begin to dislike and lose confidence in us. We will very likely see a change in the wrong direction.

In both instances, thinking only of the Love Group or taking on the Hate Group directly, we've missed the mark. We have failed to address the group in which we have the greatest chance for making a positive change. We've ignored the sixty percent of the group that started out neutral, and therefore persuadable. And if we took on the Hate Group directly, we've given them more reason to hate us and irritated the twenty percent who originally loved us. Let's now consider how we can learn to successfully relate to all three groups.

Suppose you are a manager who is speaking to a group of employees about your pet project. Before you even stand up, you should mentally divide the employees into the three smaller Swing, Love, and Hate groups. You'll also need to plan an appropriate set of messages and tactics to reach each group. Unless you do, there will be many people who won't hear what you want them to hear. Incredibly, unless you are very careful in the way you try to reach the three different groups, you will find that many members of each group will "translate" whatever you say into what they want to hear. The messages these people make up depend on their attitudes coming into the group meeting. People in the Love Group make up positive messages. People in the Hate Group make up negative messages.

This phenomenon of people interpreting messages based on preconceived ideas can be seen in a study in which loyal Coca-Cola drinkers watched a Pepsi TV commercial and loyal Pepsi drinkers watched a Coca-Cola TV commercial. When the viewers in both groups wrote down what they could remember about the ads, many of the Coca-Cola drinkers said the Pepsi ad communicated that Pepsi is primarily for kids. This was a phantom, not a message communicated openly or covertly in that ad. Conversely, many of the Pepsi drinkers said the Coca-Cola ad communicated that you can't escape Coca-Cola . . . again, not a message contained in the ad or hoped for by the ad's writers. Neither group said they particularly liked the commercial they had watched. Obviously, each group came into the test with a particular bias against the soft drink they didn't like. The challenge facing every leader is to identify the people in the Swing and Hate Groups and get them to take off the preconceived or negative lenses they are using and allow you, the leader, to replace those lenses with a set of positive ones.

In the same study, researchers next switched the exercise around. They had loyal Coca-Cola drinkers watch the Coca-Cola ad and loyal Pepsi drinkers watch the Pepsi ad. This time each group, now talking about their favorite product, had great things to say about the ads and the product benefits they saw. In an odd but unmistakable repeat of the phantom messages reported in the first research test, many positive product characteristics the viewers described were not shown or even implied in either commercial. As leaders we must remember that Love and Hate groups see the world through very different sets of lenses. The Swing Group, on the other hand, sits on the proverbial fence trying to decide which way to jump, or perhaps not caring to jump at all.

CAUTION: DON'T UNDERESTIMATE THE POWER OF THE "HATE GROUP"

No matter who we are, how good our reputation is, or how effective the hype, every group we stand in front of will have at least one disagreeing (and disagreeable) skeptic. And sometimes the group may even include a very vocal heckler. Overlooking the potential harm of the Hate Group is always a big mistake.

Consider the experience of an associate who works for Acclivus, one of the country's top management training firms. The company puts an extraordinary amount of emphasis on in its name because the name reflects their business mission. Quoting from company literature, "Acclivus is Latin for moving upward, symbolizing our purpose and commitment to partner with clients to help them reach their business objectives through the development of each individual's maximum potential."

Attempting to continue their "move upward," Acclivus invited a well-know business guru at the height of his popularity to their headquarters to make a presentation about leadership and highly effective management practices. Ironically and unfortunately, his presentation on effectiveness was not very effective. During his presentation, he repeatedly mispronounced the company's unique name, saying "Acclivious," (like "oblivious"), a simple but costly mistake. The Hate Group quickly capitalized on the speaker's faux pas and went to work undermining the speaker's viewpoints, ideas and recommendations. What a shame. Many people within Acclivus formed the opinion that the speaker came across as insensitive and arrogant. They reasoned that if they could not get excited about the man, certainly they could not get excited about what the man had to say.

On a much larger scale, in the early 90s, The American Plastics Council launched a highly successful advertising and public relations campaign aimed at saving the industry from repeated attacks by the news media and special interest groups. But like most great successes, the success of the Plastics Council came only after a few stumbles.

In the late 80s and early 90s the plastic industry's business environment was becoming difficult and uncomfortable, partly because of heightened concern that plastic was damaging to the environment. Many state lawmakers were considering legislation that would have banned or at least severely limited the use of plastic packaging for consumer goods like soft drinks and other grocery products, because of the throwaway and landfill factors. Plastics were becoming unpopular in society at large and many important customers in the automobile and packaging industries were beginning to "de-select" plastics. Leaders in the plastics industry felt the pressure. Too much manufacturing capacity was idle. Demand was down and dropping.

During the height of the crisis, a team of marketers and chemical engineers representing leading plastics manufacturers and plastics users got together in a large conference room in Bloomfield Hills, Michigan. Their conversation went something like this. "If the public just knew the truth about plastics, how it saves resources and energy, how it is being recycled, how it is getting stronger and more durable, how it makes automobiles safer and more economical to operate, there wouldn't be such a problem with the public criticizing plastics. If the public just knew the truth about plastic rather than listening to the vocal minority that criticizes it, everyone would love the industry."

After some discussion, the committee decided that they needed an advertising campaign that would get the public to "take another look at plastics." The campaign would lay out the true story of plastics and silence the Hate Group on points of resource usage, recycling, and environmental impact. In the following weeks, messages were developed, storyboards were approved, and several ads were produced. The ad agency did their job well. The production value of the ads was very high and millions of dollars of prime media time was purchased. With all the pieces of the "know the truth" strategy in place, the ads were aired and after several months, national surveys were conducted with great anticipation to track the improvements in public attitudes about plastics.

The results of the first round of tracking surveys, however, were disappointing. On the positive side, people were noticing the Plastics Council's ads because advertising awareness percentages were growing at a good pace. On the negative side, none of the measures of public attitudes were improving and some of the measures were actually turning downward. To make matters worse, reports were coming in from the field describing problems that the advertisements were creating.

A story reported by the news media in the Northwest told of a man who got into a fight with the manager of a recycling plant. After seeing one of the Plastics Council's ads that stressed how "millions of plastic bottles are being recycled each day," he loaded all of the plastic bottles he'd been saving for years into his car then drove to the nearest recycling facility. The workers at the facility told him that they didn't recycle plastic. He argued back that they must recycle plastic because he saw an ad on TV that said they did. A wild and frantic fight erupted in which the man threw bottles out of his car and the plant manager threw bottles back into the car. Finally, the determined recycler broke the plant manager's arm by slamming it with his trunk lid as the manager was trying to throw bottles back into the car's trunk. Local newspapers eagerly printed this and other unfavorable stories about the unavailability of plastics recycling. Not long after, Attorneys General from at least a half dozen states began actions to sue the Plastics Council for false and misleading advertising.

The Plastics Council quickly learned that the Hate Group can be very strong, that its members won't easily go away, and that Hate Groupers have a knack for refashioning "truth" to hurt rather than help a cause. The mistake made by the Plastics Council's "know the truth" campaign is the same mistake made by so many leaders, past and present, when dealing with tough issues and tough audiences. We, as leaders, are impatient. We want to tell our side of the story. We try to attack the problem and the Hate Group directly. It's very hard not to react. We want to set things straight. And by doing so, we usually get set straight by the Hate Group, which can only make matters worse.

MAKE THE "LOVE" AND "SWING" GROUPS YOUR PRIMARY FOCUS

Fortunately, there was a happy ending for the dilemma faced by the Plastics Council. They found and used the key that often unlocks the door to success with tough issues. That key is simply focusing on the positives embraced by the Love Group. Certainly, people love an organizational challenge for a number of important reasons. If we can uncover the reasons and find ways to help the Swing Group see the challenge through their loving eyes, we can make progress even in the most difficult situations.

Let the Swing Group See You through Loving Eyes

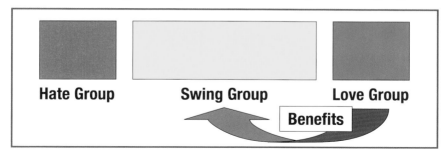

The shell-shocked Plastics Council took a brave step back from their initial difficulties to reassess what people really liked about plastic. They found that it is the material's uses in personal safety and healthcare that best highlight the noble qualities of plastic. And so, back to the drawing board.

In the next flight of ads, the American public, whether skeptical, neutral or favorable towards plastics, learned from the Plastics Council accounts of successful hip replacements, shatter-resistant bottles, football helmets and shoulder pads, cleaner water, and baby incubators. You may remember these ads or have seen similar ads pointing out the benefits plastic offers society. The success of the "Plastics Make it Possible" ads, coming after a near meltdown of the plastic industry's first promotions, is evidenced by the fact that similar commercials are still playing today and that the industry is stronger than ever.

It is as if the Plastics Council went to members of their Love Group and asked them to tell a personal story about when they first fell in love with plastic. We actually asked this question once in an executive seminar and a young man in the back of the room pulled out a picture of his premature baby. He said that he fell in love with plastic when the incubator and associated hi-tech gear, made of plastic, saved his young child's life in the hospital. That's powerful stuff.

Once the Plastics Council learned to talk to the Swing Group, using the experiences and point of view expressed by the Love Group, their ad campaign became very successful. It was recognized by the advertising industry with a David Ogilvy Gold Medallion in 1997,

Something so precious is worth protecting

I wish I could keep him a baby forever, but I'll settle for keeping him still and protected. Because he's already got big plans, and that plastic car seat won't just help keep him safe, it will give his dreams a chance to come true.

How have plastics touched your life?

American Plastics Council

Plastics make it possible
www.plastics.org

© American Plastics Council

"Plastics Make it Possible"

Once the American Plastics Council created messages targeted to the Swing Group based on why the Love Group loved them, rather playing defensive to the Hate Group, public attitudes towards plastics improved.

but more importantly, it shifted the public attitude of tens of millions of households. Today, no legislation is pending that would adversely affect the plastics industry and demand has reached unprecedented heights. With the ad campaign, the industry has created the necessary time to make the "behind the scenes" changes to substantively improve industry-wide programs in recycling, product reuse, and resource reduction.

The Plastics Council campaign demonstrates how important it is to remember leadership's first immutable law. Leaders must remember, particularly when dealing with tough issues, that not everyone loves us. We must reach the Swing Group by finding effective and appropriate ways to let our Love Group do the talking for us. In moving from surviving leadership to thriving as a leader, learning how to tap into the power of the Swing Group without alienating the Love Group or angering the Hate Group will be key to success.

Law #2: You can't push people; people push themselves

Laws do not persuade just because they threaten.

Lucius Annaeus Seneca

Managers often motivate, delegate, and train employees while holding fast to the flawed belief that employees have the success of the manager in mind. For example, with a tight deadline hanging over *their* heads, many managers act as though their employees will do whatever is necessary to meet that tight deadline. Unfortunately, if the manager doesn't take personal ownership of the task and follow up on the critical details with vision and energy, the deadline often will come and go without that critical work getting done.

When managers need a high level of cooperation and performance from their employees, they always have to ask the question, "What's in it for them?" Today's workers are comfortable jumping from job to job, knowing that secure, long-term employment at a single company is a thing of the past. Consequently, managers must be ever more creative in finding ways to get the Love, Hate and Swing Groups to push themselves in the direction pointed out by management.

YOU CAN PUSH A PERSON, BUT NOT PEOPLE

The truth is many of our learned skills that can pressure single individuals simply don't work with groups. Sometimes, when working with individuals, because of our position or sheer power of our personality we can manipulate or even intimidate someone to take action. History shows, however, that manipulation and intimidation have only limited success to influence groups. Why? Because even with groups consisting of only two or three people there is power in numbers.

The second immutable law states that groups only temporarily bend to external pressure and intimidation and are ready, willing and quite capable of pushing back. Effective, goal-oriented changes in a group almost always come from within, rarely from external pressure.

Have you ever seen someone tear a phonebook in half? You can't do it unless you "fan out" the pages so that you are only tearing through one or two pages at a time. Few people have the strength to tear through hundreds of pages all at once. Similarly, we may be able to push one or two individuals into seeing things our way, but pushing a whole group is a much, much different matter. It just can't be done with much success, so please don't even try.

People 1, Executives 0

At one time, we were working with a chemical manufacturing company that wanted to locate a hazardous-waste burn facility in one of the local communities. Understandably, the community leaders were concerned. They raised some questions with the plan in discussions with corporate executives. They questioned why their families should have to suffer with the health risks of the fallout from burning hazardous waste trucked in from other states and communities. Executives working for the chemical manufacturer decided to handle the problem in a town meeting. A group vice president of the company addressed the community leaders. He was obviously frus-

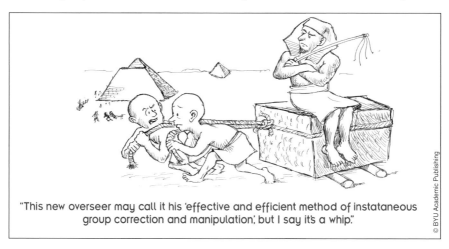

"This new overseer may call it his 'effective and efficient method of instantaneous group correction and manipulation,' but I say it's a whip."

trated with the local resistance to company plans, so he tried to intimidate the group, using the same tactics he may have used with his own office employees. A local newspaper's account of the meeting documents his approach: "I really do believe it is in your hands," he said. "I think the next twelve months at this site are going to determine whether the plant becomes a facility that will be basically squeezed down, cost reduced, people reduced, facilities reduced to a very minimal operation, or with your support, go the other direction with projects like our wastewater treatment facility and incinerator."

What he really meant and what the community understood was that if they did not accept the "burn facility," the plant (which, by the way, had operated in the community for more than 100 years) would significantly diminish its operations and lay off a substantial number of workers. The day after his speech, the executive was surprised when the community leaders didn't back down. He was even more surprised when a firestorm of local resistance was launched with the help of the environmental "watch dog" organization Greenpeace.

For that executive and the entire company, this one incident resulted in a public relations nightmare that didn't go away for more than a year. Incidentally, the plant did not later draw down its operations significantly. And to our knowledge, the hazardous waste burn facility never was built. So what seems to work in the office with one employee rarely works in front of a group. To exercise true leadership, we must use tactics that pull people together into action rather than just try to push them.

THINK MACRO-VISION, NOT MICRO-VISION

Put simply, the second immutable law says a persuasive leader who gets things done must give people a vision that goes well beyond the immediate task at hand. We all have goals for the groups of people with whom we work, but to attain these goals we must find ways to align our tasks and goals with the dreams and ambitions of the people who will be doing the work.

People often won't perform at their best unless they see the personal advantage, the old and entirely legitimate "what's in it for me?"

perspective. On the other hand, a typical manager often believes that completing a task is in itself fulfilling and rewarding. Both the employee and the manager have unique "micro-visions," that is, they can only see far enough to visualize their own self-centered goals.

Many managers try to motivate by appealing specifically to individualized goals, or micro-visions. They may offer workers the hope of special recognition, promotion, or improvement of on-the-job skills. They may try to make workers feel that they are "letting down" the company if they don't stay late, take on that extra assignment, or go on that business trip everyone else is trying to avoid. This is short-sighted, because those managers really should be talking about macro-visions. Simply put, macro-visions are goals that embrace both the company's aspirations and the personal ambitions of the individuals in the group. The macro-vision creates stronger motivation than micro-visions. Not many people can get excited about low-level goals that don't reach much farther than the task.

Here's an example of what we mean by the difference between managing with micro-vision versus managing with macro-vision. We have spent many years working with companies that operate huge customer service centers full of phones, with hundreds of employees answering customer-service questions. Working in one of these centers is not a glamorous job. For most employees this sort of job serves only as a temporary stopping place on their way through college or up the employment ladder to earn more money and gain more responsibility. We all understand that being a customer-service representative is just a job, not a career. Consequently, it is amazing how many of the companies we've worked with feel they should be able to keep the same employees in the same jobs for most of their working lives.

One of the best companies of this type that we've worked with achieves levels of customer service that are head and shoulders above its competitors. The biggest secret of their success is in their job interviewing process and new employee contracts. The recruiter begins job interviews by asking prospective candidates to write down what they want to achieve over the next few years. In general, typical goals would be finishing college or moving up into a management position. Interestingly, the company seeks out employees who have higher goals than simply getting a regular paycheck. The candidates, after writing down their goals, are then asked to come back the next day. While they are gone, the company recruiter develops plans with local colleges and company schedulers that allow these people to reach their goals and at the same time meet the staffing needs of the company.

During the second interview the recruiter hands out contracts. The contracts specify how the company will help employees meet their goals if they agree to join their team and help the company deliver the highest level of service quality in the industry. The contracts also include the date they will be hired and the date they will be fired. For example, if it takes three and a half years for them to complete their college degree, they will be fired in three and a half years. Thus we see a good example of an organization aligning the goals of its employees with the goals of the organization . . . in other words, leading with macro-vision rather than micro-vision.

On the surface, one might think the approach of writing a contract about "being fired the day you are hired" would create a feeling of job insecurity, but it doesn't. Management is using a macro-vision to transform the mundane job of customer service into an important steppingstone to a better life and career. In short, the company goals and employee goals run parallel to each other. They are congruent. Managers have found a way to hire talented and motivated employees, then help these employees recognize that company resources and day-to-day on-the-job goals are just steppingstones to help them achieve what they want most for themselves and their families.

MOTIVATING WITHOUT PAYING MORE MONEY

An important article[3] on this kind of motivation was written by a psychologist who had worked with Mary Kay Cosmetics back in the mid 80s and early 90s. At the time, the company was suffering through a twenty percent decline in sales over the previous two-year period. An exploration of company records found that the key driver of the decline was the sharp drop in the number of sales consult-

---

3.   *A Means-End Chain Approach to Motivating the Sales Force: The Mary Kay Strategy* by Reynolds, Rochan, and Westberg.

Mary Kay's mission is to enrich women's lives.

We will do this in tangible ways, by offering quality products to consumers, financial opportunities to our independent sales force, and fulfilling careers to our employees.

We will also reach out to the heart and spirit of women, enabling personal growth and fulfillment for the women whose lives we touch.

We will carry out our mission in a spirit of caring, living the positive values on which our company was built.

ants over the same time frame. The company went from a high of over 250,000 sales consultants in 1982 to only about 100,000 sales consultants in 1986. Company officials saw the problem and launched a research program to understand why so many people were leaving Mary Kay (known for its founder's habit of giving new pink Cadillacs to its top salespeople) and why so few new people wanted to join the Mary Kay sales force.

The psychologist discovered that women who became the cosmetic giant's sales consultants had five distinct personal goals—(1) financial gain, (2) being one's own boss, (3) having more time to spend with family, (4) achieving greater self-confidence and independence, and (5) attaining greater self esteem by broadening personal horizons. The psychologist also discovered that most of the women leaving Mary Kay focused on the first two goals, financial gain and being one's own boss. On the other hand, women most likely to stay with Mary Kay focused on the fourth goal, achieving greater self-confidence and independence. Based on the findings, the psychologist recommended emphasizing the ability of the job and its training program to lift women to greater levels of self-confidence and personal independence while reinforcing the positive values of the company. Earnings potential and the opportunity to run one's own business were not emphasized. A test of the new focus was conducted with several hundred women. Company managers saw recruitment rise by over forty percent through use of the new recruitment approach, so the program was rolled out company-wide. During the next six years, the number of sales consultants increased by threefold and annual sales revenue increased from under $300 million to roughly $400 million. Clearly, providing a macro-vision of what the job could do for a person and the company beyond the money they could earn had a huge impact on the company's bottom line.

Compare this approach to that taken by managers who only dole out small hourly raises and incentives. Managers who tap into the personally relevant long-term goals of their employees will be much more successful in getting people to perform up to their full potential. It takes a macro-vision of meaningful achievement to motivate people to work hard at all those mundane things that must be done, but which no one really wants to do.

Law #3: People on pedestals make easy targets

To knock a thing down, especially if it is cocked at an arrogant angle, is a deep delight of the blood.

George Santayana

Managers make a big mistake by trying to look infallible, all-powerful, and all knowing. Often it appears as if they go out of their way to violate the third immutable law. The higher we climb on our pedestals, the more tempting it is for people to knock us off. We are always surprised at the number of managers, administrators, and especially teachers who want to live out their lives as the biggest ducks in a shooting gallery. It is just human nature, whether it's in an ultra-modern company or in a medieval castle, to be tempted to take a shot at or just resent anyone riding a high horse. People just can't help it.

Leaders must be visible, vocal, and dynamic, yet they must also stay off the high horse, apart from the other ducks in the shooting gallery and at a good distance from the pedestal. This, despite the leader-in-training's noblest plans to maintain the common touch, becomes harder and harder, the more successful one becomes. The higher we climb as leaders, the more difficult it is for us to connect with those around us. And if and when circumstances or our own errors cause us to slip and make that inevitable fall, only an ability to connect with people will save us from that previously mentioned leadership spiral of death.

Perhaps you've experienced a "trust fall" once or twice during your life. If you haven't, imagine yourself on the edge of a speaker's platform, turning your back to a group of unfamiliar people who are standing below to catch you, and then letting yourself fall backwards off the platform, trusting you will connect with the people and not the hard floor below. It's an unnerving activity, and it is this quality that makes it such a popular tool in business seminars and class-rooms. We feel tremendous relief when our fall is stopped—not by the unyielding floor six feet below, but by strong and capable cradling arms.

Most people who do the "trust fall" admit they are filled with anxiety as they prepare mentally and start to fall backwards. We instinctively sense the danger of helplessly falling backwards, having only the hope that others will save us from serious injury. Most managers, however, have no such natural instinct about the critical "we're all in this together, and each of you is just as important in your own way as I am" aspect of leadership. The leader who willingly climbs up on the pedestal, feeling they deserve such prominence because they are "showing the way," "leading by example," "setting the standard," "displaying confidence," "elevating performance," etc., has not learned the lessons taught by just one trust-fall experience.

That same type of manager, on the other hand, may become sensitized to the problem inherent in "climbing up on the pedestal," and learn how to correct that weakness in his or her own nature. One such self-taught manager once shared a personal story with us that vividly illustrates this. Unilaterally, he decided the marketing materials used by his company were "horrid." He was tactful enough to keep the word "horrid" to himself, but he later admitted relentlessly pushing the other managers with questions like "how can we make this more effective?" "why are we telling our story like this?" and "what do you think we can do to improve this?" until he was personally satisfied with the results. He later realized that his constant pushing had made himself vulnerable. He had created hard feelings by setting himself up as an advertising expert and undermining the efforts and credibility of his marketing staff. In looking back at the incident he said, "I think a better approach might have been to help someone from the marketing staff come up with the idea to improve the materials and then to encourage the idea and help them move it through the development process."

Good leadership requires foresight and patience. Plus-One leaders take the higher ground, not the higher position. We must quickly see the correct path, and then find ways to allow others to find that same path and lead us along it. The concept of "staying off the pedestal" is fundamental to the cultures of China, Japan, and much of the rest of Asia. As noted by the Chinese philosopher Lao-Tzu, "A good leader is best when people barely know that he exists. Not so good when people obey and acclaim him. Worse when they despise him. The best is like water. Water is good. It benefits all things and does not compete with them. It dwells in low places that all disdain."[4]

Making the transition to exceptional manager from outstanding employee always takes time, hard work, and plenty of patience. This is a good time to review in brief leadership's laws of self-preservation to maintain your enthusiasm and momentum long enough to build your personal leadership-for-success skills.

Not Everyone Loves You. Within every group of people you will encounter and work with are three segments. We call these segments the Love Group, Swing Group and Hate Group. Based on Pareto's Principle and born out in our own experience, twenty percent of your employees (Love Group) accomplish eighty percent of the work. Whereas another twenty percept of your employees (Hate Group) cause eighty percent of the problems. The remaining sixty percent, the largest of the three segments is the Swing Group. Depending on what you say and do the Swing Group can join with the Love Group to support you or join with the Hate Group and oppose you. You

4.   Lao-Tzu (604-531 BC)

must learn to tap into the power of the Love Group, jump-start the enthusiasm of the Swing Group, and minimize the negative impact of the Hate Group.

You Can't Push People; People Push Themselves. When managers need a high level of employee cooperation and performance they always have to ask the question, "What's in it for them?" Today's workers are comfortable jumping from job to job, knowing that long-term employment at a single company is a thing of the past. Consequently, managers must be ever more creative in finding ways to get groups to push themselves.

People On Pedestals Make Easy Targets. Managers make a big mistake by trying to look infallible, all-powerful, and all knowing. The higher we climb on our pedestals, the more tempting it is for people to knock us off. It is human nature to resent anyone riding a high horse. People just can't help it. We need to find ways to stay off the pedestal. The higher we climb, the more difficult it is for us to connect with people. And when we slip and make that inevitable mistake, only our ability to connect with people will save us.

Plus-One tactics

This book is about tactics—tactics that everyday leaders can use in everyday management situations encountered around the office, home, or community. When used appropriately, these tactics can help just about anyone multiply their persuasive power. You don't have to win the special genetic leadership lottery to acquire a touch or two of a natural-born leader's charismatic charm.

Earlier, we identified three main sub-groups found within any organization–the Love Group, Hate Group, and Swing Group. We'll associate the color red with the Hate Group because they can stop

Traffic Light Leadership!
Chapters describing tactics use a traffic light to signal who the tactic is designed for. A red light is for the Hate Group, yellow the Swing Group, and green the Love Group.

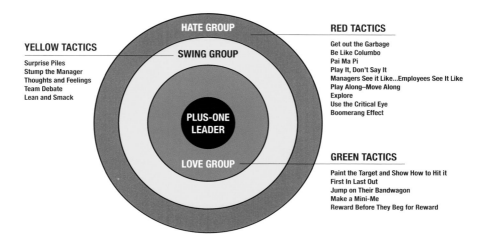

us dead in our tracks, just like a big, red stop light, especially the kind that stays red for a very, very long time when you are late for an appointment. The Love Group is like the green light, inviting us to speed forward with confidence and pleasant thoughts. As the name implies, with the Swing Group things can go either way, just as with a yellow light. If we use caution and time our plans just right, we can still move forward with the Swing Group and make great progress before the light turns red. If we fumble around without a good tactical plan, the light may turn on us before we're ready and bring us to a screeching halt.

Knowing which tactic to use and when to use it will be an important topic in this book. We developed each tactic to work best with each group of people. We'll discuss some of the red tactics geared towards surviving the Hate Group first. Then, we'll discuss those tactics that can help us energize and then tap into the power of the Swing Group and send them our way. We'll also describe a powerful set of "green tactics," those that can help us keep our path free and clear of any obstacles. Each of the tactics we'll explore and where they fall—red, green, or yellow—is summarized in the chart above.

Before we jump into the tactics, we'll spend a moment discussing four basic leadership styles. This will help you adapt the tactics to your own personal style and leadership situations.

Chapter TWO

ARE YOU A NATURAL BORN LEADER?

This book outlines many tools and tactics that can help us become effective leaders. However, we can know all of these tools and tactics and still struggle unless we understand enough about leadership's four basic personal styles, where we fit within those styles, and how to best adapt our personal style to whatever leadership situations we are given.

In his play *Henry V*, Shakespeare points out the qualities of a great man who is capable of wining great battles. What is special about Shakespeare's King Henry? Is the man remarkably strong, benevolent, clever, or ferocious? Or does he have some other remarkable quality? How can Henry accomplish so much when his royal enemies by comparison accomplish so little? Shakespeare's answer is simple: Henry's mindset.

The night before the decisive battle at Agincourt, King Henry walks disguised through his camp talking to his soldiers, trying to understand what they are feeling, what they fear, and what they hope for. In stark contrast, the French nobles spend the night among themselves, bragging about how grand they are and how easily they will trample down King Henry and his pathetic English army.

On the morning of the battle, King Henry speaks to his men not as a king, but as a brother. The army can feel his deep respect, his personal commitment, and his love for them and their country. They know he holds them dear. They believe that dying for King Henry and winning the day for England would be better than cowering com-

Shakespeare's King Henry V

A great man capable of winning great battles. Does he have the ideal leadership style?

fortably at home. The rest of the story is history. Thousands of French nobles gallop forward to their deaths. Their cause is lost. The English win the battle and the war with only one hundred Englishmen killed. According to Shakespeare, King Henry wins the day with his mindset. Mindset is a powerful multiplier. Shakespeare's King Henry is in every sense a Plus-One leader.

Every leader reveals his or her mindset by the particular style that person relies on when managing others. Models of communication classify style by looking at a leader's degree of forcefulness and sociability[5]. In our research, we find that communicating with sociability and forcefulness are both important to successful management. This 20th century discovery wouldn't surprise 17th century Shakespeare. He portrays King Henry as a man who not only knows what he wants, but as one who stands out in his ability to get close to his soldiers.

The four basic communications styles match up with how we go about managing others. We call the four styles, "dish out," "give in," "robotic," and "win over." The Dish Out style is predominantly forceful with very little or no sociability, whereas the Give In style is predominantly sociable with very little or no forcefulness. The Robotic style is neither forceful nor social. The Win Over style is forceful

---

5.   *Selling Today* by Manning and Reece

The Style Grid

The four basic leadership styles can be visualized on a two-by-two grid.

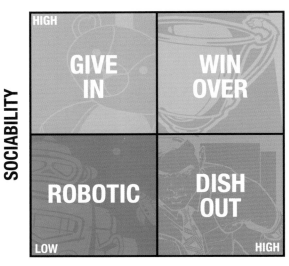

yet markedly social. We will explore each style in detail. You might even ask a good friend to read the descriptions and let you know where you currently fit in. You will probably find that another person, especially a significant other, is much more accurate and free of bias than you are in identifying your personal leadership style.

Dish Out

You cannot push anyone up a ladder unless he is willing to climb himself.

Andrew Carnegie

A friend was once working on a research project in France when a colleague took him to lunch and ordered a meal. When the food arrived our friend noticed that the salad was a little different than

Fois Gras, France

Foie Gras in French means "plump liver," a term used to describe a goose or duck liver. This choice fowl from the Perigord region is fed specified types of corn in abundance, which accounts for its unique flavor. Foie Gras should be cut into thin slices immediately prior to serving. This will allow its extraordinary rich flavor to be preserved.

anything he'd seen in the U.S. Aside from the usual greenery, some nasty-looking stuff that looked and smelled a little like meaty paste accompanied the salad. The American researcher, being a good sport, tasted it and asked his host, "Umm, this is very different. What is it?" "Goose liver," his friend replied, quickly adding, "I'm glad you like it. Let me tell you how it is made. The goose is put in a very tight cage so it can't move. Then a funnel is used to keep pushing food down its throat into its stomach. We feed it three times the amount of food a goose naturally eats in a given day. This causes the goose's liver to get much bigger and taste much better!" Hearing this, our friend sat there, somewhat stunned, and then blurted out, "Who would ever think up doing something like that?" His colleague, not fully under-standing the somewhat negative tone of the question, smiled broadly, raised both of his arms and cheerfully announced, "the French!"

A manager with a Dish Out style wants to put people in a cage and relentlessly push rules, details, and tasks down their throats. A Dish Out manager wants to force people to gain bigger and better abilities. This leader may mean well, but the pushing can be so hard that some employees may fight back, which can cause other employees to become negative and join the battle against the leader. It is easy for a person using the Dish Out style to lose the support of almost everyone in the group.

For example, a student once told us about one of the low moments in her college education. "I was so excited to take this course in economics," she said, "because the professor was a world renowned expert in his field. Everyone in the department said he was brilliant and that he was sure to win a Nobel Prize for economics. There is no doubt he was a genius, but frankly I had a hard time staying up with his relentless lectures, I think he assumed we all knew some things that we didn't. So," she continued, "I went up after class one day to ask him if I could come by his office to talk about some concepts that were difficult to grasp, and then he shocked me. 'If you're having trouble keeping up,' the professor told me bluntly, 'I suggest you go hire a tutor.'"

People say that often they walk out of a Dish Out experience feeling as if they've just been fed with a fire hose, kicked by a steel-toed boot, and/or whacked by a two-by-four. A teacher or manager using the Dish Out style is very concerned with saying everything they have to say, but they rarely slow down long enough to make sure everyone is comfortably following along. In the Dish Out leader's world, employee comments must be quick, correct and to the point so that the leader can make more time for what he wants to say.

"Before he joined the company as vice president for policy development and training, he raised geese for gourmet French restaurants."

© BYU Academic Publishing

Consider the following comments describing a Dish Out manager. "We never worry about it that much when he asks a question. If we just wait a minute or two he'll answer the question himself, but the trouble is he just talks on and on until we lose interest. We remember when we were working on a project with a manager from another business team. In our group meetings he wouldn't let the other fellow say one word. It was funny, because here is this one team leader waving his raised hand back and forth to make a comment about the project and our manager just kept on talking and talking."

"Well," we say, "it sounds like the manager is sincere about wanting your business to succeed." The employees reply, "He's sincere and he knows his stuff, but he makes us feel overwhelmed and awkward when we don't do everything he asks us to do and if we don't see the world exactly the same way as he does." "It is clear that he values results over people." Often people adopting the Dish Out style are very good followers. But as leaders, unfortunately, they can come across as intimidating and harsh even though they have many good qualities. Evidently, what works well for stuffing geese doesn't work as well for leading people.

Do you think you might be relying on a Dish Out style? There are two distinct varieties of Dish Out leaders. If you are a natural "teller," you may make people feel as if they are incapable of doing much of anything on their own. You believe you must prod people into action. If you are a natural "seller," you may consider people to be pawns on your giant management chessboard. You act like people are easy to manipulate and that they should be willing to rely on you to show them what is best for them. To get their cooperation to do whatever you ask, you promise employees something that they desperately want, but you may have little or no intention of ever delivering. Both of these approaches, while effective in some situations, rarely evoke the passion, inner drive, and endurance needed by employees who are expected by their leader to work with him or her to achieve extraordinary results.

Give In

Cautious, careful people always casting about to preserve their reputation and social standing never can bring about a reform.

Susan B. Anthony

A person with a Give In style appears to be a much kinder and gentler soul than a person using the Dish Out style. The Give In person can get close to people. Such a person is generally seen by others as one who wants to please them. Some might even consciously or subconsciously categorize that person as a "pooh bear." If co-workers feel their assigned task is too hard, they may look to Give In to make it easier. On a university campus, a student who fears he or she will not do well in a necessary course frequently will seek a class taught by a known Give In professor. A Give In will always suggest several ways in which the worried student might raise a low grade. In the business world, a Give In manager will give employees time off whenever they ask for it, leaving the other, more responsible employees to fill the gap.

Many people intuitively recognize and take advantage of a Give In leader and the Give In usually knows he or she is being manipulated. However, one consistent trait of the true Give In is that he or she would rather gain the approval and acceptance of co-workers than risk disapproval from them by requiring office discipline and fair performance. When an individual can't handle rejection, anger, and objections to his or her ideas, giving in to the objectors rather than finding effective ways to gain cooperation can easily become the norm. And this can often shut down the effectiveness of an entire organization. The chronic Give In would rather get a little accomplished, without any argument or grumbling, than "push" dynamically, which would be extremely uncomfortable, possibly lose the "good old boy" acceptance of colleagues, and perhaps accomplish nothing at all.

In spite of its virtues in keeping everyone content, "pooh bear" habits can sap the energy and drive of a company's best employees. They can be left feeling like the older brother of the prodigal son. They reason, "Why should I work hard when the complainer at the next desk gets away with doing less and still gets rewarded?"

Recently, a colleague mentioned that he was pleased by the way student teams were working out in his class, but some students were concerned about having to individually answer the questions from a case study for the final exam. He explained that "The students wanted me to let each team take their final exam together rather than individually. I said it sounded like a great idea to me and gave in. Do you think I did the right thing?"

Students like this professor, but few are truly committed to what they learn from him. They rarely take what he says very seriously, they admit, because "mostly everything he tells us is just common sense." At the root of their attitude is the feeling that "pooh bear" words do not need to be respected. How can they take seriously anything from a person who has so little commitment to their own plans, goals, or ideas? The common perception is that this person is just telling them what they want to hear and letting the "lazy" ride the coattails of the "hardworking."

It is common in our modern, "give in to get by" culture for most people to be polite, sometimes even noncommittal, when discussing a manager or professor with a Give In style. To their credit, such managers may actually do some good by keeping people happy, or helping an organization to function without too much management-employee conflict. Every individual should cultivate some of the qualities of the classic Give In leader. However, we should emphasize "some" in that last sentence. Based on several years of interviews in universities and corporations, we find that the Give In leader rarely produces peak performances or experiences in those around him or her. We believe in the long run that exclusively relying on the Give In style can create a sense of lost opportunity in both follower and the leader. Looking back, it is not unusual for "pooh bears" to lament, "woulda, coulda, shoulda."

Robotic

Some people talk in their sleep.
Lecturers talk while other people sleep.

Albert Camus

It's easy to visualize a Robotic manager. Just recall an instructor in a college math class or an engineer with a parabolating-supercomputer-for-a-brain who has become a manager. The Robotic style leader excels with a sometimes bewildering array of facts and related, if arcane, data, but appears detached and aloof when dealing with people. Such apparent detachment can be disconcerting to employees, although delving deeply into the Robotic individual's psyche one would usually find that person is actually flesh and blood, and really cares about others. As an instructor, the Robotic typically arrives early to fill the chalkboard with the day's quota of solutions, formulas, proofs, and theorems. There's little discussion, little apparent concern for questions or difficulties, and even less eye contact. The Robotic quickly leaves at the end of the class, spending more time with the contents of the ubiquitous briefcase than with any human in the same room.

In general, people who have a Robotic style actually like other people, but they are more at ease with numbers or abstract concepts. Robotic managers believe that good employees are just as Robotic as they are. From their point of view, a "good" employee is self-programmed to solve problems and get work done efficiently. The Robotic manager enjoys working things out without input or interruptions from anyone else. So, that individual naturally reasons, "Everyone else should do the same."

As one might imagine, an individual with a Robotic style does not often get a chance to manage others, because established management, whether it's in industry, corporations, or academia, usually favors the individual who easily interacts with everyone, rather than the person who turns down an invitation to lunch because there's some abstruse formula that needs tweaking. This is unfortunate, because the typical Robotic individual is so gifted, bright, and willing to invest tremendous personal time and energy to get a difficult job done right. The problem is the Robotic person who doesn't self-medicate with a little of the social Give In and forceful "push" mental skills when dealing with others, leaves employers, colleagues, and potential employers with the usually false impression that the "robot" doesn't care about them or the business.

Win Over

Leadership is the art of getting someone else to do something you want done because he wants to do it.

Dwight D. Eisenhower

We have found in our ongoing research that some individuals with Win Over personalities are "made" that way over time by circumstances and personal effort, while some just come that way out of the wrapping. But whatever their particular variety, Win Over people strongly connect with people as a by-product of getting others to fully embrace what they have to say and what they want to accomplish.

Let's think about that for a moment because it is an important point. We find that employees admire supervisors when employees enjoy how they are being trained, what they are learning, what they are doing, and what they are becoming. Certainly, the Win Over manager is a good person, but that's not the only reason why people want to listen to them and work hard for them. People respect what a Win Over leader has to say because that leader somehow projects a feeling of commitment to their goals, programs, and policies and has respect for what others think. Equally important, the Win Over leader shows a willingness, maybe even enthusiasm for creating experiences that help others feel the excitement of winning together.

Several years ago, filmmakers at Brigham Young University produced a documentary film that told the story of a renowned professor who for many years taught Shakespeare to undergraduate students. He used a unique method to get his students to fully experience and appreciate the power of Shakespeare. Rather than taking a broad and shallow approach to Shakespeare's large body of works, he selected a single scene from the play *King Lear* to serve as the text for the entire semester-long course. Students started out by reading the scene and learning the meaning of the new vocabulary words and strange-sounding Elizabethan-era English phrases. Next they each took a role in acting out and recreating that scene. All along the pro-

King Lear
Courtesy of Shakespeare's Globe Theatre, London 2001.

fessor talked with them about the meaning of the words and the kinds of emotions people would be feeling in the scene. As he answered their questions, he shared events from his personal life to help students feel the adventure of exploring his unique world of knowledge, ideas, and experiences. As a final step, even though none of them had any previous acting experience, the students performed the scene for a movie crew.

In the documentary, the filmmaker compares the student's portrayal of the King Lear scene with one professionally acted and produced by the BBC, as well as those produced by prominent American movie studios. Personally having spent a lot of time in London theaters watching Shakespeare, it was remarkable to plainly see that the student performances were in many ways better than all of the professional portrayals. However, it was even more remarkable to think about how much the students had learned about Shakespeare and to witness the lasting impact this Win Over leader was having in the lives of so many young people.

While the format of his class was certainly entertaining, the professor's end goal was not to entertain. The students admired and appreciated the professor, but the end goal was not to be admired and appreciated. It was not to make each student in the class remember for life that one scene from a Shakespearean play. The end goal of that professor, and the Win Over leader, is to invite people to share in the tremendous excitement that can permeate a project when people work together to discover new worlds of ideas and actions, and participate in worthy accomplishments.

Embrace, then enhance your personal style

In general, people go through life using, in greater or lesser proportions, the four different personal styles described above. These styles match up with how people prefer to get things done and relate to others. The four styles, Dish Out, Give In, Robotic and Win Over, all exist in some kind of balance, usable or disabled, within each of us. People are least responsive to the Robotic style and most respon-

The Wizard of Oz
Each of us can contribute in our own special way.

sive to the Win Over style. However, each style has its merits. Remember that in the great old 1938 Judy Garland classic movie, *The Wizard of Oz*, it took the Tin Man, Wizard, Scare Crow, and Lion working together to get Dorothy Gale back to Kansas.

Each style is a combination of how others perceive our degree of interest in accomplishing a project, as compared against our personal interest in connecting with people. With a Robotic style, people see us as having very little interest in either. With a Win Over style, people see us as having a great deal of interest in both. Dish Out managers only demonstrate interest in achieving a measurable goal. Give In managers only demonstrate a real commitment to connecting with people. Of course, just because you tend to rely on a particular personal style does not make you a good person or a bad person. Each of us has a style that we have adopted, for better or worse, according to our natural, hard-wired talents and abilities as flavored, dampened, or otherwise formed by specific circumstances in our individual lives.

Research, and our own personal beliefs based on many years of study and interaction with all types of leaders in many types of situations, indicates to us that great leaders are great because they can either consciously or intuitively adapt their style of leadership to the needs of the situation at hand. In one sense they engender all of the best qualities of the four styles.

1. They know their data and facts (Robotic).

2. They are results oriented (Dish Out).

3. They like to get close to people (Give In).

4. They make work rewarding for everyone (Win Over).

Each of us must recognize, accept, and embrace the person who we are right now. Then, knowing the "who" of our persona, and knowing that each of us can and should become capable of leadership in our personal lives, in our careers, and in our communities, we can figuratively roll up our sleeves to insert into our own "who" elements each of the four styles of leadership, depending on what's lacking, while trimming the over-abundance of less-needed elements already within us. Each style offers a foundation upon which to build. If you naturally use a Win Over style, you are fortunate, because you are starting with a stronger foundation than the majority of people around you. For the rest of us, developing into a natural leader may prove to be a very unnatural process. It may be uncomfortable and may even "turn people off" until we get the knack of leadership. This is life's primeval urge, to remain comfortable and in some kind of mindless harmony with the flow around us. This is not leadership. To disregard one's own potential, especially after all four leadership styles have been placed before us like a free buffet, is to adopt a "good enough" mentality and outlook, with the all-too-common consequences: low self-esteem, low energy, and perhaps even dissatisfaction with life itself.

But once we understand where we are right now, we can move on and upward to become more able to master problems as they arise around us, more skilled at recognizing the best qualities in those around us, and more effective in every effort as we master the proper mindset, principles, and tactics of Plus-One leadership.

We have talked at length about personal leadership styles and the three immutable laws of self-preservation. It is time to start talking tactics! In the next four chapters we introduce four essential tactics designed to ensure we survive the Hate Group. We call these tactics Get Out the Garbage, Be Like Columbo, Pai Ma Pi, and Play it–Don't Say It.

Chapter THREE

GET OUT THE GARBAGE

---

*Pay attention to your enemies, for they are the
first to discover your mistakes.*

Antisthenes

Have you ever noticed that when you are trying to get an important point across to a group of people, there are almost always several people in the meeting who are smirking and quietly whispering to one another? If you have, you've just found your Hate Group. You may confront them, but invariably they will claim that they're not talking about you or your point, but you know they are. All of us have been distracted by these behaviors. In our experience these sidebar conversations are nearly always about how our approach, ideas or presentation style doesn't "measure up." We call the phenomenon a counter-argument. Making claims always brings out counter-claims.

It's a fact of life for some individuals to be difficult and opinionated, regardless of whether the topic is increasing market share in a global economy or just tomorrow's weather on the golf course. Consumers often counter-argue an ad when faced with information that goes slightly contrary to their view of the world. Advertisers also know that when consumers counter-argue an ad that the selling

"The term refers to 'mental' garbage, Jonesy."

points in the ad's message simply don't get through. Counter-argument is often caused by negative mental images that people carry around like old leather baggage. Such negative baggage is rightly referred to as "garbage." If you don't take out the garbage, it spoils everything you do. It smells things up. It gives power to the Hate Group to slow your momentum. Getting rid of the garbage is not just a good thing to do, it is essential to your success as an effective leader. Getting rid of the garbage will give you a clear understanding of the barriers, minefields, and battlefields you will have to deal with and work around in order to be successful in achieving your goals. Remember, it is hard to fix things and avoid pitfalls that you don't know anything about.

Collecting the garbage

Consider the following example. It's based on experiences we've had when conducting seminars on professional selling and negotiating skills. At the outset, we usually ask everyone to name some things that come to mind when they think about selling. For the first few minutes, people will say nothing at all or they will say something that they think we want to hear, like, "selling is a professional career" or "selling is a way to make lots of money." After a few minutes we clarify that what we are really looking for are the "top ten answers given by 100 average Americans who were recently surveyed." This simple approach apparently releases everyone's inhibitions. They can say many of the negative things they are thinking because the goal is now to guess what other people have said in the past. Now everyone really opens up and the garbage starts coming out.

The most frequent responses are, "Selling is a profession where you must lie to succeed" and "Selling is a pushy job." One of the most unique statements we ever received from this process was provided by a young woman who said, "Selling is like being a prostitute where you sell all your values and morals for money." Our response to that comment was "Wow, we've never heard that one before." Sometimes it is very hard to just be an observer of the process and not a judge of the participants. It's not easy to avoid becoming defensive. However, we must force ourselves to smile, play along, and obediently write down all the negative statements and misperceptions. If you react defensively, the "game" will end abruptly and the group will freeze up. Then, unfortunately, the garbage will remain locked inside, waiting for just the wrong moment to surface and undermine all your preparation and hard work. Being defensive about negative comments also gives your Hate Group ammunition to take potshots at you when you least expect it.

Dealing with negative baggage

A leader must learn, after collecting the garbage, how to throw it out of the minds of employees so it does not contaminate our ability to move our efforts forward. Actually, throwing the garbage out is the easy part, compared to showing patience and empathy, while biting one's tongue during everyone's complaints and negative comments. There are several different ways to start dealing with the garbage. Some ways may work better than others, but this depends on the situation, the nature of the group and the leader's own personality. Also there is a lot of latitude to be creative in such a situation. For example, to deal with the negative stereotypes of professional selling, we may say something like this. "After all, look at the facts! In professional selling, the average yearly amount spent in the U.S. on training a person right out of college is about $40,000. In contrast, the average amount spent on training a retail sales person in the United Sates totals less than $5." Unfortunately, most people's perceptions about professional selling are closely tied to their experiences dealing with retail and door-to-door salespeople who seldom have any professional training. Therefore, most people learning for the first time about professional selling skills can't help but bring along a lifetime of biases, negative baggage,and misperceptions. These biases and stereotypes can keep some of the best people from considering a career in professional sales, which is still one of the highest paid and personally rewarding careers. Perhaps even worse is that negative perceptions about selling seriously detract from the careful listening and genuine learning that we hope will take place.

Of course there are other approaches. One colleague writes all the positive comments he collects on one side of a blackboard and all the negative comments that come out on the other side. He then "crosses out" all of the negatives and says, "I completely agree with what you're saying, if I ever start doing or talking about these sorts of things please stop me." The group then sits back in their chairs feeling a little stunned as he continues by saying, "We are only going to focus on the things on the positive list, so let's just stay as far away as we can from all this other stuff." If you can do something similar with the groups you work with then our sincere congratulations. You've just disarmed your detractors and erased many of the reasons the group may have had for not listening to you.

Another way to start dealing with "garbage" is by playing a game we call "refuting the critics." Here, members of the group are asked if they can refute the criticisms that the Hate Group has brought up and which we have then listed for all to see. We don't say whether we believe those listed negative comments are true or false. As we step through each negative comment or perception, we ask for people to try to "refute the critic" and for others to "defend the critic." This is an invigorating exercise for the group. In our example, many people start by saying things like, "My mother or father is a salesperson for a major corporation and they don't lie to succeed." Others will chip in, "I know salespeople who are very professional in dealing with customers. They are not pushy at all, and their customers wouldn't stand for it." Another person will say something like, "Professional selling is much different than retail selling. Most of you are thinking about your experiences in dealing with people who go door to door or sell used cars." When there is not much left to discuss we clean up the scraps, if there are any, and move on to the list of positive comments. We reinforce the validity of the positive comments about selling and say—you guessed it, "As we learn about professional selling, we will spend all of our time talking about these things." Often, we also add a few more positive items to the list in order to give everyone a better scope of what we'll be doing over the next few days in the training seminar.

OJG: On-the-job garbage

In a day-to-day business setting, the "get out the garbage" tactic plays out in a remarkably similar way. One manager writes, "Today I had Al, our chair-frame production lead, walk into my office. He said he and several others in chair-frame production were going to quit if we went through with a management change we were planning. We wanted to ask Jim, our chair-frame assembly manager, to manage both chair-frame production and chair-frame assembly. Al said Jim was a yeller and intimidator, and often threatened his employees to get them to meet production quotas. While I thought that Jim wouldn't behave like that, I organized a group meeting of the framing department to get out the garbage.

People expressed their concerns and opinions. There were some examples of Jim's hot temper, but for the most part Jim was simply guilty of telling rather than asking. So rather than making the management change right away, we took an interim step. First we gave Jim some mentoring sessions to prepare him for the new responsibilities and have put him on a three-month track to gain the respect and ultimately take over management of the additional department." The manager reports that the overall result of getting out the garbage has been very positive. The employees working in chair-frame production and assembly feel respected and none have quit their jobs. A young interim foreman has stepped up his performance and shown great potential for the future . . . and Jim is developing into the kind of strong leader everyone thought he could be.

Map the "mindfields"

It takes about 15 minutes to start the process of getting out the garbage. But really this is only the first short battle of what is usually a much longer war. Hang on to the "garbage list" of issues. We refer to these items as "mindfields." The items are sure to pop up again and again. We spend a lot of time thinking about the list because we want to find safe ways around or over these mindfields as we work with people. Getting out the garbage gives us a "heads up" and starts us down the right road with less negative baggage to carry. Consequently we are much more successful "winning over" people and getting them to buy in to our vision. It gives us a way to understand the key arguments that the Hate Group may use to influence and build support with the Swing Group. As a reminder, the Swing Group always makes up the vast majority of people with which we work. Success with them will determine our overall success.

The steps for getting out the garbage are outlined below. It is one of the most important tactics managers can use. Letting a negative attitude mature and ripen as you go about your business with a pair of emotional blinders on is more than dysfunctional; it is suicidal. It stops the listening, learning and doing that must go on to operate a successful business. As a negative attitude ripens and then spoils, it begins to smell. In turn, the bad smell drives away many potentially good performers and performances. It is better to tackle negative perceptions and stereotypes from the start rather than leaving it to struggle with later on. Some issues you can quickly sweep away. Some issues require consistent, long-term effort. However, once you start getting out the garbage you may find—like we have found over the years—that the process becomes addictive. We feel compelled to do it because we can't stand the thought of letting all that old garbage smell up our hard work and planning. We don't want the Hate Group to limit our opportunities to positively influence our business or the lives of others.

Identify the mindfields before you step on them. Draw out thoughts about what you want to do before you do it. We often like to play games such as Top Ten Answers or Refute the Critics to gather and address the "baggage" surrounding an idea or project. The tactic allows us to (1) identify Love, Hate and Swing Groups, (2) discover issues or concerns that could undermine the success of a project, and (3) avoid doing or saying anything that will hinder our ability to effectively lead.

Steps for getting out the garbage

1. Ask what thoughts or feelings come to mind when saying the task, goal, or topic. If all the comments are positive, ask them to put on a critical hat for a moment or have them play the Top Ten Answers game.

2. Write down and highlight the negative and positive issues that are raised. It can be hard, but play along without being defensive. You are an observer not a judge.

3. Ask the group to play the Refute the Critics game by finding ways to refute and/or defend the criticisms that you've listed. You should not attempt to attack the criticisms yourself. That won't help your cause. Focus efforts on reinforcing the positive items.

4. Assure everyone that they will be focusing on the positives and not on the negatives.

5. Make a written or mental list of the key negative issues brought up. These are the mindfields you'll need to defuse over the long haul.

Chapter FOUR

BE LIKE COLUMBO

---

*When you soar like an eagle,
you attract hunters.*

Milton Gould

W hen great communicators really want people to listen and take action, they find ways to present complex topics in simple ways, using simple words. The right words can be powerful weapons for change. For example, legislators couldn't muster enough support to revise the severe estate tax laws until the estate tax was labeled the "death tax."

Columbo © Universal TV

Leaders who are great communicators also seem to have a knack for asking questions and giving answers in a humble and almost self-effacing way. We say this disarming tactic is to Be Like Columbo. It is named for the unassuming TV detective named Columbo, portrayed by Peter

Falk in the hit detective-drama series of some years ago. Columbo has unkempt wavy hair, wears a dirty trench coat that looks two sizes too big and smokes a stub of a cigar that looks as if he found it in a gutter on the way to the crime scene. While Columbo has a way of talking and asking questions that most people interpret as being sim- pleminded, he always solves the case and it is usually because the "smart and clever" guys reveal things that they never intend to. In Columbo TV episodes, the smarter the criminals are, the harder they fall.

Adopt a pressure-reducing attitude

It has been our experience that people find greater success in life when they act more like Detective Columbo than when they act, for example, like Sherlock Holmes. Trying to be the world's greatest "anything" really turns up the pressure. It reminds us of a story about a pretty good golfer who was trying to tell a "beginning" golfer in his foursome how to hit a difficult shot over some water to a small green. The beginner looked at a wide and intimidating creek running in front of the green then looked back to the other three members of the foursome. He then looked directly at the expert and said, "Wow, what club do I use to hit this shot?" "How do I hit the ball so that I can get it over the water, but still stop the ball on the green?"

The expert enthusiastically explained the shot, telling the novice which club he should hit, and how the ball needs to go high so that it stops quickly on the green. "Don't even think about all that water," he said, "it's not difficult, just think about your target and make a good swing." "Here, I'll show you how to do it!" The expert then teed up his golf ball, made his swing, and—you guessed it—dropped his shot right into the middle of the creek. It was quite a performance for the beginner and the two other interested spectators. By acting like the expert, he put too much pressure on himself. In the clinch, he couldn't perform. Then to make matters worse, the beginner stepped up and hit his shot safely over the water and right onto the green. Ouch! The sting of humiliation! The message we have for lead- ers is that it is good to be a giant, but please find ways to be an unthreatening, humble giant. Any other way increases pressure, increases defensiveness and ultimately crushes one's ability to effectively lead.

Be Like Columbo is the tactic we think of when trying to stay off that dangerous pedestal discussed earlier, and when trying to protect ourselves from the Hate Group. Consider this example of how to implement the Columbo tactic. A professor from a well-known northeastern business school was lecturing on the basic principles of finance to an audience of entrepreneurs and other business professors. "Today we are going to talk about some important principles of finance," the professor started off. "These are (1) you can't run a company without cash, (2) it is better to have more cash than less cash, and (3) it is better to have cash today than cash tomorrow."

He then described each of the principles using several homespun stories and simple diagrams. Towards the end of the presentation a man sitting with his arms folded in the back of the room, obviously a representative from the Hate Group, spoke out on behalf of his colleagues. "I thought we were going to be learning about how you teach entrepreneurs about finance," he blurted out. "How can you teach finance without numbers?" "We were expecting so much more." "How are we supposed to answer the tough questions that get asked about the underpinnings of the difficult analysis tools like discounted cash flow and net present value?"

The finance professor smiled and said, "Well I usually try to dodge the tough questions, but I'll try by doing something like this." He then turned and filled the blackboard with the mathematical formulas and proofs that went along with the financial principles he had taught that day. His intricate, quickly written chalk formulas included all of the "numbers" associated with discounted cash flow and net present value. He understood the importance of expressing difficult concepts in simple terms and only reluctantly took on the role of expert and even then with self-depreciating humor. When living in a world of experts, success is not determined by how much you know, but by how you choose to say it.

How to be like Columbo

As we have already said, we believe it pays in the long run to be a Columbo instead of a Sherlock Holmes, even if the goals of both are the same. One manager recently shared a story about the marketing team leader at his company. This leader patiently came up through the ranks in the company and learned every element of the business and the customer. Her understanding of the market and ability to execute an effective communications campaign was unmatched in the company. Yet, every time the spotlight headed in her direction, she cheerfully deflected the praise towards members of her team. The manager noted that one could never guess that she was applying a tactic, because her behavior was completely sincere and heartfelt. Of course, everyone likes attention, but she discovered that she could feel just as loved by generously sharing praise and the center of attention.

Another manager used the Columbo tactic to diffuse a potentially tense situation. She sent out an email to her staff outlining the time and purpose of a meeting she wanted. In a quick and angry response, one employee demanded a better explanation for why she would take him away from "real work" to go to the meeting since all meetings were just a useless waste of time and effort. The employee said he wasn't deliberately trying to be obstinate, but that he didn't see a need for something so unimportant, especially when his old boss had never held such a meeting.

After thinking for a while and coming up with a plan, the manager meet with the employee in person and began by saying, "I'm not quite sure what your position is. Were you for or against the meeting?" The employee then laughed so hard that he forgot about being upset regarding the proposed meeting. He ended up thanking the manager for being so understanding after he had responded rashly.

It is ironic that so many of the popular self-help books on public speaking stress the importance of establishing credibility by demonstrating expertise. The advice seems so logical. In our experience, however, setting yourself up as the World's Greatest Expert is like painting a target on your chest and handing out shotguns to employees. It creates a string of counter-arguments in the minds of most listeners. It gives the Hate Group juicy opportunities to knock you down from your perch. It makes the Swing Group ask questions like, "Is he really talking from personal experience or is he just repeating something he read in a book or heard from some consultant?"

Or people may even think, "He says he is the expert, but what he is saying doesn't match up with what I know to be true." Being the expert puts you under tremendous pressure and often requires you to fight to defend your authority and position. Eventually the pressure to perform at such a high standard can only result in delivering poorer and poorer performances. Experienced leaders usually deal with their expertise in a self-effacing way. They find simple ways and simple words to express their ideas. They give themselves "wiggle room." They never try to make themselves look completely right and consequently are never completely wrong.

Therefore, don't be the leader who is always right. Just be like Columbo. Relieve some of the pressure of leadership by disarming employees rather than arming them. There is nothing smarter than acting "country dumb." Play down expertise. Don't present your ideas and or thoughts as if they are rare treasure. Learn to guide and prompt employees to discover the appropriate goals and vision to move the company forward. Learn what others know and have to say before sharing what you think. Be a guide on the side, not a sage on the stage. Consider the following ideas to be like Columbo:

1. Listen more than talk, and when you must say something make sure it is primarily to ask others what they know or what they think.

2. Try to get other people to answer the hard questions for you even when you already know the answers yourself.

3. If you must demonstrate expertise, try to interject some self-effacing anecdote about how hard it was for you to acquire the expertise.

4. When someone gives you a compliment, reply with enthusiasm, gratitude and a simple thank you. Then find a way to pass-off that compliment to someone else.

Chapter FIVE

PAI MA PI

> *To conquer the enemy without resorting to war is*
> *the most desirable. The highest form of generalship*
> *is to conquer the enemy by strategy.*
>
> Ancient Chinese Warlord

ong Kong is a beautiful and exciting city. At least part of the beauty and excitement comes from having lots of people creatively packed into a very small space. Some residential sections of Hong Kong have a population density estimated at nearly 60,000 people per square kilometer, nearly double the population density of Manhattan [6]. In fact, many cities in China have staggering population densities. It has been like that for a long time, too. Perhaps these extraordinary conditions have given rise to some extraordinary skills. Obviously, the Chinese know something about getting along with the people around them. They know how to survive and be happy in circumstances that are often crowded, tough, and unpleasant.

Pai Ma Pi, literally "pat horse bottom," is a bit of Chinese advice for dealing with people that have power to either hurt you or help

---

Pai Ma Pi

Is more than simple flattery—it's recognizing and appreciating specific personal victories of employees, especially difficult employees.

you. This is an apt description of the Hate Groups lurking in just about all the situations we face as leaders. Pai Ma Pi isn't simple and obvious flattery, although it is sometimes translated that way. It is much more challenging to pull off. It is something that must be done with finesse and delicacy or, as the Chinese say, you may end up Pai Ma Ti, that is, "patting the horse's hoof." It is easy to praise or recognize employees in the Love or Swing Group, but the tactic really comes to life when it is used on the Hate Group, those we would prefer not to talk to in the first place. The magic of Pai Ma Pi is that it can turn around problematic employees and nudge them closer to the Love Group. As leaders, we must learn to dig deep to find exemplary actions of difficult employees. Even storm clouds have silver linings.

Father and son reunion

Recently, a father shared a personal story. "This weekend I woke up early and began to do some yard work. When I came back into the house to grab some tools, I could hear my 10-year old son downstairs playing Nintendo. Like most dads, I thought to myself that he should be outside helping me, but I knew if I just flat out asked for his help that he would complain and ask why he always has to do it. Then I'd force him to help, he would begrudgingly put in a half-hearted effort and I would get angry at him. So, without saying anything I went back outside and started working again. But as I worked, I got an idea on how I might use Pai Ma Pi. I went back inside and watched him play the Nintendo for a few minutes, told him how good of a Nintendo player he was, then told him I had a problem. I told him that I was working in the yard but wasn't making much progress. I told him he is so fast that I knew with his help I could catch up and get the work done quickly . . . then a moment of truth; I asked him if he would mind helping me for a while. He shocked me by saying okay. He just wanted to make sure he could continue to play Nintendo when we were done. For the next hour and a half he worked hard and cheerfully, and we both had fun. I was amazed."

Being specific leads to sincerity

Managers often make weak and ineffective attempts at using Pai Ma Pi. In our part of the country, they will indifferently listen to what an employee has to say, then, while walking briskly away, offer an insincere "preciate cha." We should want to praise people at every opportunity, and that praise should be the outcome of observation and sincere appreciation for what employees are doing. Anything less invites the horse's hoof. A leader's praise works wonders when it is

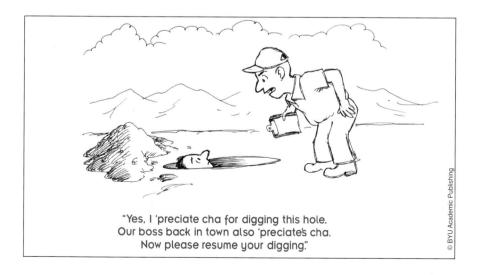

"Yes, I 'preciate cha for digging this hole.
Our boss back in town also 'preciates cha.
Now please resume your digging."

© BYU Academic Publishing

specific. Unspecific, insincere praise only harms a leader who offers it. This is particularly true for the leader working with the Hate Group. That group is suspicious of any praise coming from our direction. On the other hand, they can't resist the spotlight when it draws attention to something they believe they have really done well.

For those of us having no natural leadership ability, how can we train ourselves to give sincere praise? It can be difficult to develop that particular skill to become a natural reflex action where appropriate. Seeking an answer to the question, we gained some insight from a presentation given by a well-respected psychologist specializing in marriage relationships. His simple formula for marital bliss: "Treat your partner as if they are giving you the best they have." Depending on the situation of the moment, the partner may be giving their best or giving something less than their best, but if the other partner assumes the best is what's being offered, then finding ways to empathize with and praise the partner will be easy.

The Hate Group has power to do great harm, or if they choose, great good to any project. They can frustrate leadership or provide everyone in the group with a tremendous sense of accomplishment. Our advice in dealing with all employees, but particularly the Hate Group, is to "pat the horse's bottom." Look for every opportunity or even create opportunities to praise the Hate Group. We use these opportunities to get closer rather than distance ourselves from difficult employees. However, it is imperative that we praise specific behavior that the Hate Group has done and is proud of. A quick "pre-ciate cha" is counter-productive. Of course, it doesn't hurt to generously praise specific contributions made by everyone in the organization. When you show confidence in others, they will have confidence in themselves. But showing confidence and having high expectations are by themselves not enough to attain peak performance. People perform their best when they know their performance is noticed and means something. Most people, whether leaders or not, need to learn to praise others more generously. To that end, we suggest always treating people like they are giving their very best in the situations they find themselves. Maintaining that attitude helps us spontaneously say the right things and keeps us out of a lot of trouble at work and also at home.

Chapter SIX

PLAY IT, DON'T SAY IT

---

*Money was never a big motivation for me,
except as a way to keep score. The real
excitement is playing the game.*

Donald Trump

Free-spirited baby boomers, Generation X slackers, and now the Entitlement Generation who fiercely resist making the transition from child to working adult[7] . . . every group of workers seems to have their own idiosyncrasies and offer their own challenges to management. On the other hand, one thing each of these generations holds in common is that they are all heavily into "fun." In today's business world, if work isn't relevant to the employee, if hard work isn't generously rewarded, and most importantly, if the work isn't fun, then the employer can count on apathetic, underperforming employees and a high turnover.

With today's skeptical attitudes about work and employers, an organization's Hate Group is a formidable foe to leadership. The group easily enlists recruits and attracts deserters. Managers will not produce positive results unless they do much more than just tell employ-

---

7.   *Ready or Not, Here Life Comes* by Dr. Mel Levine

"Who's ready for some Leadership Games?"

© BYU Academic Publishing

ees what needs to be done. Managing has never been harder, more frustrating or more fixable. There are no easy fixes, but one approach we strongly recommend is to substitute some clever, attitude-changing, "We're all in this together" games for all the droning, hopeless lectures that are sure to fall on deaf ears and make even the most enthusiastic employees check their watches. In other words, Play It, Don't Say It. The success of this tactic is based on the fundamental truth that leadership is really about moving motivated people from one activity to another, and not about lecturing one employee after another about why they should be motivated.

A classic example of Play It, Don't Say It was once described by world-famous motivation expert Dale Carnegie.[8] He tells the story of a company executive who is looking for ways to improve the productivity at one of his factories that is seriously underperforming. The solution is elegant and effective. The executive walks out on the factory floor and asks how many production runs were completed by the shift just coming off the line. He then takes a piece of chalk and writes the number on the factory floor. As the next shift of workers arrives, they ask what the number is. When they find out, they

---

8.   *How to Win Friends and Influence People* by Dale Carnegie

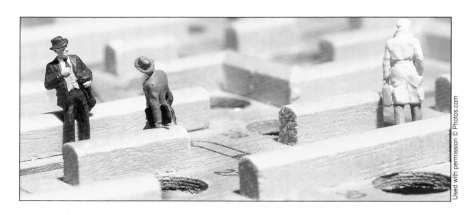

Used with permission © Photos.com

say that they can beat the number and do, then scratch through the first number and write down their own. The third shift does the same thing. Within a short time that factory is the most productive in the company.

Perhaps all this sounds too good to be true, just some Dale Carnegie hyperbole. But we have found plenty of creative managers out there who have convinced us that inventing clever games for employees can and does increase their productivity and job satisfaction. We couldn't help but laugh at how the tactic is being used by a customer-service manager at a local company. To make the tedious work more fun, each day she asks the service associates to work a random word, such as "hotdog," into all their service calls. Employees love it and at breaks and after work they spend time laughing about how they used the random word in the day's customer-service calls.

The variety of such games is unlimited. One manager got excited about Total Quality Management and consequently formed a committee that met every other week to discuss ways to use TQM in the company's procurement process. Energy for this type of committee meeting is usually low in American businesses[9] and the company's Hate Group was in usual form. As the manager launched into an explanation of why he wanted to start the meetings, he was greeted with a roomful of blank stares and sidebar conversations. He quickly stopped the lecture and started playing a game. He went to the black-

---

9.   *The Stuff Americans are Made of* by Hammond and Morrison

board and asked, "What do you hope our competitors' procurement departments are struggling with?" He got lots of responses and listed all sorts of funny things as well as relevant things. The manager ended the meeting early and said that he could see their procurement department struggling with some of the same issues and wanted to use the meetings to give the committee opportunities to address the problems and make some meaningful contributions to the company. The committee members felt energized and interested!

Today's workforce has built up a thick communications callus when it comes to absorbing lectures and instructions. Managers can say it, but employees won't necessarily hear it, much less do it. Our modern lives are filled with so many distractions that it is the rare person who will listen carefully or respond well to instructions. Therefore, when you really want to get a point across, invent a game to get the point across for you.

We often use games having something to do with competition. Everyone likes to win so people will usually pay close attention and put out extra effort to get a victory or make a meaningful contribution. While natural born leaders may be able to invent games on-the-spot to encourage teamwork, enthusiasm and extra effort, the rest of us perhaps are not nearly so clever. We can, however, match the natural born leader's instantaneous cleverness by investing more time determining exactly what we want to accomplish, and then planning appropriate team-building games in advance.

Team building with planned or spontaneous games may be difficult in the corporate atmosphere of some organizations that seem satisfied with status quo. This, of course, doesn't mean that doing things a little differently, with humor, friendly competition and original thinking, won't be appreciated in the executive suite(s) if it results in measurable improvements and increased profitability. A good rule of thumb policy is that the "stodgier" and more complacent an organization is, the more important team-building through innovative, possibly even silly little games, can be to kick-start the organization into a fresh perspective about its goals, while also pumping employees full of new ways of looking at what they're doing and why they are doing it.

Even a natural born leader might have an uphill struggle when developing team-building games and exercises appropriate to both the company and to the problem or situation being addressed by those games. To overcome corporate resistance to the team-building by games concept, the manager might start by amassing a little research on the subject. Contact managers from other similar or larger-sized organizations and ask them about their own experiences in this area. Ask about the kinds of planned and/or spontaneous games used, and why, plus any other data that might strengthen your case for experimenting with a few games of your own.

And remember, while every out-of-the-box effort entails a certain amount of risk, its possible that your best, most original efforts take your organization to new levels of success. However, when devising a game, remember that "less is more." This means games should be low- or no-cost (at least at startup). If you sense that a game has energy and builds enthusiam, then improve it and repeat it.

Start by determining what you want to accomplish (or what you perceive the organization wants to accomplish). More productivity? Greater employee efficiency? Better customer/client relations? Better communications throughout the organization? Those are all important, but start with just one and avoid headaches trying to come up with a single activity that covers all the bases. It can't be done.

Use ideas generated from examples shown in this book, from examples gathered from other sources, as long as they are successful and appropriate to your organization's "personality," and adapt as necessary. And try also to come up with games and learning activities that are entirely your own.

Team-building activities, simple, spur-of-the-moment games or more complicated activities, do work. They can revitalize an organization that has slowed down a little, and push a more successful company up to even greater heights!

Part TWO

Seven Principles to Make a Habit

Part TWO

SEVEN PRINCIPLES TO MAKE A HABIT

To a person browsing the "self-help" section of a bookstore or library, it might seem as if everyone who has ever led a group of Boy Scouts up a gentle incline, organized a successful yard sale, or been involved in business, industry or academia has something to say about modern leadership. A quick internet search shows that there are hundreds, if not thousands, of books, tapes and CDs, and uncountable leadership lecture tours on the market, all offering management insights and secrets of key leadership principles.

You will notice that in this book we describe nineteen tactics to *start* readers down the path of self-motivating, individualized, and truly effective leadership. While so many of the available leadership materials dwell on generalities, we try to stick with "how to" tactics. Nevertheless, before moving on to describing more tactics, even we need to pause and outline the principles on which the tactics rest.

So what's so special about seven, and what makes these specific principles of leadership so different? Experience at all levels of management, and lots of it. From ground floor all the way up to the executive suite. And we are relieved that there has been more success than failure on every level. Hard-earned success gained from discovering, testing, and learning the efficacy of seven key principles. Seven, as used here, isn't a magic number. We all know about Snow White's Seven Dwarves, some history buffs may recall the famed (and fictional) Seven Cities of Cibola, and there are numerous other places in history, ancient and recent, where "seven" implies some kind of mystical significance. For us, it just happened that our wide-ranging experiences in observing leadership, distilled and organized for the benefit of others, includes seven basic principles of special interest to the Plus-One leader. In other words, we really couldn't think of eight.

These seven leadership principles have enormous power to either make or break a leader. Our principles establish a framework for the four tactics that we have already outlined as well as for those that follow. Aside from being connected to tactics, they are also important in helping leaders adopt a believing mindset, which we discuss in Part 3 of this book. By embracing the believing mindset, Plus-One leaders gain flexibility in dealing with situations uniquely their own (as most managerial situations are), and give them the mental insights necessary to develop their own unique set of successful, workplace-friendly tactics. The seven principles are not ends unto themselves, but should function as wellsprings for new ideas. We have used the principles to generate 19 tactics. We hope to hear from readers who produce new tactics to address challenges they face!

The seven critical leadership principles we will be discussing in the following chapters are:

1. Take the high ground. There will always be conflict in a dynamic organization. Focus on solving issues, not on attacking personalities or position.

2. Connect when you correct. Recognize the fact that not everyone gets it right every time, and use mistakes to draw closer to people, not push away from people.

3. Provide an escape route. Make your point but allow your opponent to leave with dignity and confidence unshredded.

4 Lead like you pray. Before asking for new help praise past contributions.

5. Consider a kind question. Rather than telling, try using a carefully thought-out question to help others "see the light."

6. Carrot is better than stick. Hold both but use the carrot much more frequently.

7. Make the journey using switchbacks and stepping stones. Marching straight up the mountain and reaching the top by yourself is not leadership, it is a disaster.

Chapter SEVEN

TAKE THE HIGH GROUND

People who know the least always argue the most.

Unknown

I n the Roald Dahl movie classic, "Matilda," the little girl's father, Harry, tells her, "I'm smart; you're dumb. I'm big; you're little. I'm right; you're wrong. And there is nothing that you can do about it."

A lot of movie-goers wanted to hiss when they heard this line. It was a cold and meanspirited statement, and there will always be people around who talk to their employees just like that. And that kind of management doesn't keep its good employees very long. It is undignified and misguided to attack the person instead of discussing

Matilda © Columbia TriStar

Don't be Harry!

Telling your employees "I'm smart; you're dumb. I'm big, you're little. I'm right; you're wrong. And there is nothing that you can do about it," will do nothing but fuel the Hate Group and turn off the Love Group.

the issue that causes the conflict, particularly when the manager is the "Harry" and the employee is the "Matilda." Part of a manager's job is to manage conflict, and "managing" is much different from "creating." Tense situations and conflict of any type are hard to manage because emotions, feelings, and self-image are always involved.

Not long ago, one of our colleagues quit teaching to take a job in industry. In his new job he seemed glad he wouldn't be very involved in management. He said he took the new job because he couldn't handle knocking himself out year-after-year for people who didn't seem to care about what he did for them. Under pressure from the administration to raise his teaching evaluations he did everything the teaching gurus told him. He memorized names, improved and expanded course content, and provided quick and detailed feedback. Nevertheless, after putting in all that extra work and time, his evaluations were some of the worst of his career. We suspected a problem that had nothing to do with his teaching competence. So we asked him if he had experienced any conflicts in his class. He said there was nothing major, just a student who had argued with him about how he graded a test question.

"How was the problem resolved," we probed. He replied that the student wouldn't listen to reason, so he finally told the student the way he had graded the question was right because he said it was right and that was the end of it. But of course it wasn't. That day most of his students in the class saw him become a "Harry," when he told the complaining student the classroom equivalent of, "I'm smart; you're dumb. I'm big; you're little. I'm right; you're wrong. And there is nothing that you can do about it." He had lost his temper, regardless of whether his way of grading the test was fair or not, and that was wrong, both because it showed inadequate conflict-management skills, and because of something called "student evaluations."

The other students remembered what they "heard" when it came time to write their evaluations of the instructor. All his hard work and dedication didn't save the professor, because he got defensive. He decided to protect his self-image, forgot to keep talking to the issue and started attacking the student. And that one slip-up wrote "finis" to what could have been a productive and satisfying academic career. In business, in industry, in academia, community service and even in the home, when there is a conflict, the Plus-One leader must stick to the issue or else risk seriously damaging their ability to lead.

Managing conflict

Conflict cannot be avoided in a dynamic office or workplace. It is the inevitable by-product of people working together and experiencing pressure to get the work done. But, allowing small conflicts to grow unchecked makes it nearly impossible for a team to work as an effective unit. Conflict stops people from participating, and while we may never get 100% effort all the time from every person, in our competitive world, we need 100% of our people contributing.

With the heat on to get work out the door, human emotions flare up, frequently at the most inopportune time. If the work group is feeling the wrong emotions, the project causing the pressure will usually teeter on failure. On the other hand, if the work group is feeling the right emotions, the project, regardless of difficulties, can often become a grand success.

Plus-One leaders take the management high ground when directing frustration and/or anger away from people and focus attention on the concern or issue.

Cushioning and Directional Questioning

Employee

Manager

ISSUE

Direct attention at the issue and away from each other!

The first step in making workplace conflict an experience that builds instead of destroys is to cushion the employee's frustration by acknowledging it: "I can understand your concern," "I think anyone in your situation would be concerned." Or simply mirror the expressed concern with an understanding nod, saying, "Sure, I can see that."

Next we help people focus on the concern or issue by directional questioning, e.g. by suggesting, "Tell me more about it," or asking, "Why is this so upsetting to you," or "Why do you think that this sort of thing is so very frustrating for people like us?" Then, finally, we talk about various ways the issue has been resolved in the past and/or commit ourselves to finding a solution. That way management is perceived as respecting the employee's view of the problem, being appreciative that the employee has brought it up, and that the problem will be examined so that the project can move forward and the conflict will be resolved before it festers and grows.

In Part 3 of this book, we introduce the tactic, Managers See It Like...Employees See It Like..., plus the tactics known as Play Along— Move Along and Explore. These tactics give managers proven ways to get people talking directly to the issue and not arguing with the individual. Everyone wants to use tact when dealing with conflict. We find that the more tactics we master, the more tact we have.

Chapter EIGHT

CONNECT WHEN YOU CORRECT

Pay no attention to what the critics say.
Remember, a statue has never been set up
in honor of a critic!

Jean Sibelius

Most of us have never experienced hard, demanding military service, but—thanks to movies, books and friends who have—we can all conjure up in our minds the sounds and images of boot camp. We can see the short haircuts and the military fatigues, and who can forget the tough, heartless drill sergeant? He is yelling! He is in our face! He takes no excuses! He is reshaping us whether we like it or not. We know that real-life military drill sergeants, despite their reputations and rough on-the-job demeanor, must have families, and so we can imagine it must be tough growing up around one.

We once asked a friend whose father was an Army drill sergeant what his home life had been like. He didn't want to recall the memory, but after some thought he said his father had an explosive temper and it didn't take much to set it off. It is the life work of some drill sergeants to always be on guard for mistakes, to always look for rule breakers and slackers, and to be ready to leave unforgettable memories with those who fail to follow instructions exactly and promptly. Our friend said he thought dropping his pants, grabbing his ankles, and taking a few good shots from his dad's belt were just normal parts of growing up. He recalled that his first real father-son bonding experience took place when his father took him inside an armed military tank on the Army post and let him actually shoot its flamethrower. And this became a metaphor for their relationship. The son would push the buttons and the father would shoot out the flames. But under the khaki-colored crust, there was still a father who understood tenderness, even if he couldn't express it.

Our friend said his dad wrote a letter to each of his children shortly before he passed away. The letters were filled with regrets about missed opportunities and personal failures to better connect with his family. Developing a drill sergeant reputation in civilian life is one way to approach management if we are only working to earn a paycheck and we want to build a reputation as a tough-minded, Dish Out businessperson. But—and again, it's years of personal experience with many types of leaders and study of their overall success that's guiding us here—we believe every manager, at every level and in every kind of business and industry, must make a positive personal connection with employees to achieve consistent, career-long success on the job site.

How to connect

Even kindhearted managers know that a business office, an industrial worksite, and any other competitive endeavor aren't Sunday schools, just as they aren't boot camps for slackers. The mission of a Plus-One leader simply isn't to lovingly endorse every idea, action and comment coming from employees. People have misperceptions. People make mistakes. People blurt out bad things. It is a part of daily life we can't escape. On the other hand, multiplying negative on top of negative only comes out positive in math class. Criticism of employee effort, attitude and result is an implied part of the job description of a manager. But the biting reality of this implication can cause a real conflict between the manager's kindhearted side and his or her "get the job done" side. So how can we criticize without being critical to the point of damaging, possibly even losing the personal connection with those around us?

We can't build or maintain a personal connection with someone we are yelling at. So, as we outlined in the previous chapter, even though there may be a distinct increase in our body temperature right under our collar as we approach the employee who failed, we first must focus, focus, focus on the specifics of the *issue*, the "What do you think could have been done to prevent the conveyor breakdown?" approach rather than the "Simpson, is that your doughnut in the reactor?" personal accusation and attack.

Identifying Personal Styles

Style	Descriptors	Office Space	Likely to Ask
Robotic	Technical, Detail-oriented, Precise, Persistent, Conservative, Slow to make decisions	Work-oriented, Organized, Showing lots of activity, with achievement awards on wall	"Can I see some more data on that problem and/or solution?"
Dish Out	Technical, Goal-oriented, Workaholic, Blunt, Demanding, Impatient, Tough-minded	Desk situated to contact people across desk, achievement awards on wall, no posters or slogans on wall	"When will I start seeing some solid results?"
Give In	Liberal arts, Good listener, Supportive, Soft-hearted, Maintains status quo, Avoids risk	Friendly and open atmosphere, pictures of family displayed, personal mementos on wall	"Is there anything else I can do for you?"
Win Over	Liberal arts, Strong opinions, Enthusiastic, Fast decisions, Creative, Towering goals	Motivational signs on wall, Desk placed for open contact with people, cluttered and unorganized desk	"How would you feel about working together to get this done right?"

Secondly, we can increase our chances of connecting (and thus minimizing conflict) by recognizing and adapting to the employee's personal style. This approach is similar to the way we can categorize specific differences in leadership style. An employee, just like a manager—because they're both just people—can be identified by his or her distinct personal style: Robotic, Dish Out, Give In, and Win Over, just like management.

You will find several cues in the chart shown on page 74 that in general are useful for identifying personal styles[1] in employees.

Adapting to fit personal style

We can begin connecting with people and resolving differences by adapting what we say and do to link with their personal styles. For example, a manager named Jon described a situation in which he was sitting in his office when his boss, who had been traveling out of the country, came in. The conversation went well until a VP joined in. At that point Jon said that jet-lag must have set in because his boss starting showing off for the VP by making very negative comments about how worthless Jon was. No one likes to be embarrassed in front of a company VP and Jon felt he had to say something. He thought for just a moment and then sat back in his chair, smiled, and calmly said, "Yeah, I'm a real office screw-up. I think I'll go answer phones in the lobby now!" His remark connected with his show-off boss without sounding defensive. Later Jon received an apology from his supervisor and their relationship has been excellent ever since.

There is no need to be defensive when you are under personal attack. A defensive attitude in business, just like in nature, is a sign of personal weakness. Just think what the African veldt might be like if all those pointy-horned antelope started attacking the stalking lions. And a defensive attitude, particularly among managers, is a signal to all those "antelope" in the workplace that they've got a leader who can't lead. When you, as a manager, are on deck to respond to the comments of a Dish Out, hit back quick and hard because a Dish Out

---

1.   *The Best Seller* by D. Forbes Ley

is impulsive. With a Give In, communicate that the criticism is painful and then use words and phrases that thoughtfully explore the hurtful comments. Ask clarification questions from a Robotic and provide evidence of a positive track record, but be careful; don't overstate your performance or you'll just look like a braggart. Entertain a Win Over with some funny observations connected to the negative comments. Jon's boss was a Dish Out, so Jon hit quick and hard, but with a touch of humor and not with a defensive tone. Just the right move with just the right tone connected with the personal style of the manager.

Even in situations where most people might automatically erupt with angry disapproval, great leaders look for ways to criticize indirectly. Dale Carnegie offers a classic anecdote. He describes a manager finding two employees smoking cigarettes directly under a no smoking sign on the factory floor. Pointing at the sign, he could have lowered his eyebrows and spit out, "Can't you read? You can't smoke in here!" But instead, the manager made eye contact, pulled two cigars out of his coat pocket, walked up to the workers and invited them to smoke the cigars in the employee break area. The factory workers received two important messages: The manager is friendly and the manager wants them to smoke where it is allowed.

Response to Criticism

Style	Response
To a Robotic	Offer a Robotic an opportunity to clarify what was said that bothered you. Support yourself with evidence of good results but avoid overstating anything, which would label you as a braggart.
To a Dish Out	Hit back quickly and as hard as necessary to make your point with humor and without actually insulting the person. A Dish Out says things on impulse, without calculating in advance what the criticism might do to the recipient, and a fast response will get that person's attention.
To a Give In	In private conversation, as soon as possible after the criticism has been expressed, explain the words and phrases that the Give In used that were unfair and hurtful, and give the Give In the opportunity to—well—give in a little without becoming embarrassed.
To a Win Over	Entertain a Win Over by telling a personal story to exaggerate and "humorize" the mistake..

Being friendly without losing leadership control almost always works, but to fine tune the approach, we offer some ideas for connecting with each personal style below.

Ideas for connecting

ROBOTIC

- Ask many questions, desire information
- List advantages and disadvantages
- Be organized
- Be thorough and attentive
- Do not rush

DISH OUT

- Make points quickly
- Be firm and sure of yourself
- Emphasize "what's in it" for them
- Provide options
- Focus on goals and results

GIVE IN

- Spend time building rapport
- Support their feelings
- Minimize their feelings of risk
- Show interest in their goals

WIN OVER

- Talk about their ideas, opinions and dreams
- Skip over details
- Be funny and entertaining
- Focus on making their dreams come true

Chapter NINE

PROVIDE AN ESCAPE ROUTE

A good reputation is more valuable than money.

Publilius Syrus

Even though the definition of a "good" reputation differs from person to person, it is a fact that people will defend their good reputation down to their last breath. A person may be guilty of something, but it is human nature to deny that guilt. We can't help counter-arguing any and all criticism that comes our way. Also, it is not unusual for employees to deflect criticism aimed at them by searching for things to criticize about the manager or other person who criticized them. Yet, even though a really good manager is loath to do it, there will be situations that force that manager to pass on criticisms and other bad news, even though that manager knows doing so may well create ill feelings and fuel the Hate Group.

Minimize the downside of passing on criticisms and bad news by giving people an escape route. One of our colleagues once failed a student in his marketing course. The student made an appointment to talk to the professor about his grade. As Tom explained that the marketing course was the last he needed to graduate, the professor noticed the student biting on his nails, chewing them so short that they were actually bleeding. The professor started moving Tom

Used with permission © photos.com

Provide an Escape Route

When you sense tension, provide an escape route for employees.

towards an escape route. He said, "Tom, it looks like you've been under a lot of stress lately." Tom said there had been serious sickness in his family and pressure building up at work. The professor continued, "Tom, a big part of your failing grade is based on your peer evaluation score from your teammates. I don't think they were fully aware of all the difficulties you've been facing in your personal life." Tom nodded his head and said that he hadn't told anyone on his team about his situation.

Our colleague concluded, "Tom, I appreciate the contributions you made to the class and know in different circumstances you could have done better, but considering the situation I feel I should raise your grade to a D, a grade that will have you graduating. Will that be all right with you?" Tom was thrilled. He got the message that he personally should have worked harder and that his teammates felt he should have made bigger contributions, but he still went away happy and our colleague didn't have to fearfully look over his shoulder for Tom to get even.

Choosing escape routes

The type of escape route we create for someone depends on the situation. In the situation described above, Tom was looking for a rational way out and was happy when our colleague offered him one. When a person confronts you as a leader and needs a way out, you will sense the tension in the air.

Recently, we played golf with two friends. One was a seasoned manager, the other his boss. We had played golf with the boss before and knew that he hits the occasional bad shot and gets angry, which can spoil the fun for everyone. We eagerly watched to see how the manager would deal with his boss on the golf course. Predictably, the boss started hitting some bad shots. We could all sense the tension building in the air, but before the boss's anger could get out of hand the manager smiled and said to him, "I think you must be hitting one of those golf balls that has its center of gravity just off a bit. I've heard it can make a ball fly pretty crooked." We all laughed at the obvious absurdity of this and the tension evaporated. As the day went on more of the boss's shots sprayed left and right. We just smiled and said that he must have got a bad batch of balls. We kept the comments light and humorous and the boss's escape route remained wide and clear.

However, providing a rational way out for a person who is angry and isn't looking for one is just the wrong thing to do. It can create tension rather than relieve tension. For example, we played golf with another friend who hadn't been on a golf course for years. As he whiffed shot after shot we feared he might start feeling embarrassed, so we provided a wide variety of reasonable escape routes by remarking that it had been a long time since he had played golf, the shot was difficult for everyone, the grass was very deep, the green was really hard, etc. Finally, he gave us a frustrated look and growled, "You know what I like about you guys is that you always make up all my excuses for me." The escape routes we had offered him didn't work because they sounded like insults to someone who didn't want to make excuses. It's vital to remember that offering a person an escape route when they don't want one just "rubs it in their face." In this situation it may be best for everyone to acknowledge the goof ups and simply laugh about them.

Lower the barriers to improvement

When a person is confronted with a personal failing the natural inclination is to give up. The popular myth is that great people walk a straight upward path to success with little apparent effort and with no missteps or miscalculations. It's common for a person to reason that, "If at first I don't succeed, then I should try something else or perhaps not try anything at all." In a recent movie there's an encouraging line: "Why do we fall down? So that we can learn to pick ourselves up."

Making mistakes is not an awful part of life. And making mistakes is not the end of life. Making mistakes is a *necessary* part of life. We must make mistakes so that we can learn from them. If we are not making mistakes in our lives, then we are not really living. This fact of life has been around from the beginning (many of us may remember Adam and Eve's little problem with fruit). Knowing this makes the study of history and the great people who made history a little more interesting, and that fact should also help to make each of us more apt to learn from the mistakes we will surely make in the future.

Some managers, however, communicate a much different message about mistakes. They make employees feel that if they make a mistake, any mistake, they are not paying attention, or they are stupid, uncooperative, incompetent, and on the "short list" to get laid off. In our society a mistake carries such a strong stigma that most people go to great efforts to hide their mistakes or make things worse by putting the blame on others. This tendency to not want to admit a mistake can cause much greater damage than to simply own up to it and move on. Many people often won't even experiment with new and unfamiliar things for fear of making mistakes. Others who make a mistake lose confidence in themselves, and their effectiveness drops when doing other tasks with which they are familiar.

Much of the problem with employees denying their mistakes, hiding their mistakes, and trying to blame others is in reality caused by poor management. The employee is afraid of being embarrassed, or humiliated, or being moved to the top of that "short list" by a manager who has a reputation for short-fused leadership. Managers, regardless of whether or not they lead like a drill sergeant or are a little less acerbic but still unpleasant, need to start sending out a better, more positive message:

Mistakes are sometimes serious problems, but most are easy to correct.

An owner of a local Baskin-Robbins ice cream store shared this experience with us. One of his best employees left a freezer door slightly ajar when closing the store and much of the ice cream spoiled during the night. The employee called the owner to tell him that he felt badly about the mistake and would understand if he needed to pay for the ruined ice cream. However, the owner did something extraordinary. He said the ruined ice cream was a serious problem, but not one that hadn't happened before. He told the employee that he felt that he was a very good employee and that he wanted to sit down and have a talk to figure out how to make sure the freezer would get completely closed every night. He said he appreciated being informed about the problem and that the employee wouldn't need to pay for the ice cream.

The owner did something wonderful for the employee and his business. He found some ways to solve a recurring problem and made a good employee even better. A good manager helps the employee feel that it is easy to make corrections for most mistakes and that learning from unintentional mistakes moves the employee further down the path towards personal goals.

Hammer and heal; don't just hammer

Sometimes a situation gets so far out of hand that we want to hammer an issue hard and direct. Few moments are more frustrating and disheartening than when the manager has made every possible effort to lead a group to greatness, but their performance continues to fall short. Long after the workday has ended, the manager keeps asking, "What went wrong? Why is no one listening? Why is it such a struggle to get people to do what needs to be done?" For any leader these are dangerous thoughts. With these thoughts pounding in our heads, we might forget ourselves and blurt out things during the working day that will empower our organization's Hate Group and cripple our future effectiveness. We have seen some managers deal with poor performance by vocally hammering employees to the point where they hold their heads so low it looks as if they moved they would get carpet burns on their foreheads.

Certainly, it's true that sometimes a group performs so poorly that it needs a jolt of reality, but the wise manager knows that under those circumstances there is a need to do more than just hammer. The weak performers also need to be lifted up and put back on the right path. A leader is expected to hammer a group or an individual who is not performing up to known abilities, but a Plus-One leader will also heal the employee or group after the hammer is put away.

Here is the crucial, but often forgotten or—worse—ignored rule:

There should be no hammering without healing.

When you, as a leader, take up the hammer to meet with a group that has not produced according to a reasonable schedule, you should directly confront them and explain how disappointed you are in their performance. Tell them that you expected much more from them, that people they respect would be disappointed by their behavior. Follow up with a reminder of how the project should have been done, as compared to what their work actually produced. Now, and this is critical, after the hammering session, we recommend the group be quickly dismissed without discussion.

You, if you are on the path to leadership greatness, should then at most let a day or two go by without getting together or talking with the group. Interestingly, it is common in such circumstances for many employees to call to express their support for the manager's position or apologize for their ineffectiveness. During the next meeting the "healing" takes place. First, you should apologize for being so direct and impatient (because, of course, you were). Often, exceptional managers will even take some of the blame on themselves for letting the group down. This is important because it softens the blow and shares the responsibility. It takes a strong leader to admit being part of the problem contributing to poor performance. During this follow-up meeting the wise manager will clarify the vision of what the results should be and then reinforce a positive belief in the group's actual capabilities.

It is amazing how well this two-step process spurs people on to greater action and commitment. We admit the approach sounds extreme and it is, but we have found that it is okay to hammer as long as healing follows.

Steps in the hammer & heal

Hammer

1. *Determine*: the nature, extent, and possible ripple effect of the problem

2. *Assemble*: Identify the employees responsible for the problem and call them to a special meeting as soon as possible after the problem has been discovered.

3. *Confront*: Describe the problem and its ramifications and let the group know that they are responsible, and their mistake or inefficiency is deeply disappointing to you, personally, as well as to others in the organization who may be affected by the problem's ripple effect.

4. *Explain*: Point out in detail the seriousness of the problem (i.e. its effect on marketing, profitability, other deadlines and project plans, customer/client relations, etc.).

5. *Alternate Scenario*: Describe what positive results were expected and what could have been achieved had the problem not happened.

6. *Close*: Dismiss the group without further comment.

The Healing

1. *Call* the same group to a meeting within the next several days.

2. *Apologize*: for being so direct in the previous meeting. Accept more personal blame for whatever happened than you think necessary.

3. *Clarify*: the vision of what was expected and what can be done by this group.

4. *Close*: End the meeting on a high note, by expressing new confidence that the group will in the future perform to their highest abilities and meet your own high opinion of their potential.

Chapter TEN

LEAD LIKE YOU PRAY

Silent gratitude isn't very much use to anyone.

Gertrude Stein

Most people in the United States can repeat the Lord's Prayer even if they happen to get some of the words wrong or forget a phrase or two. It begins "Our Father who art in heaven, hallowed be thy name." This simple prayer teaches a powerful leadership lesson: Before you ask someone to do something for you, you say or do something that honors that person. It is important to build up a "bank account" of gratitude before even thinking about asking people to tackle tough assignments. We can't wait until "crunch time" to let people know that we recognize who they are and how grateful we are for the positive things they are doing for us and for the organization.

Unfortunately, many managers don't do this. They rarely take the time and effort to learn names, much less pay attention to specific accomplishments or express gratitude. We want results, not chit chat, is their mantra. Every leader wants cooperation, but too many are so wrapped up in the upward movement of their own careers that they do not think to honor those who make their leadership success possible. It's a little embarrassing to think that here in the greatest

Christian nation on Earth, so many of us have never learned the simple lessons of the Lord's Prayer. Our gratitude bank accounts are chronically overdrawn.

We once heard about how a great old church got built several hundred years ago. It highlights how the "lead like you pray" principle can impact a situation either positively or negatively. To this day, so the story goes, in front of an impressive old church in a town in Europe there's a curious-looking statue of a man with a string of bells draped around his waist. The man immortalized by this statue, with his sister, donated the money to build the church and even supervised its construction. The brother and sister grew up as orphans. They were the last children in a family line blessed with great wealth and power. While the girl was graced with a sweet and loving nature, the boy was overbearing, impatient, and outspoken. He was such a tyrant that he paralyzed people just by swaggering into a room. The sister thought her brother would change with age, but he didn't. In fact, he got worse. One day she developed a plan to help her brother get over his problem. She announced to the townspeople that she and her brother would build a great church to honor their family. The brother would supervise one-half of the building. The sister

"I appreciate your sincere concern, but just work things out and submit a report when you've completed your task."

would supervise the other half. Whichever of them finished their half of the church first would win the contest.

The brother really liked the idea. He knew he could get the builders to work hard. He knew he could win the contest. But after several months, his sister was winning. In a panic, the brother redoubled his pressure on his builders. "You're lazy," he shouted at them. "Look at how much more work they can do than you can." The sister then put the rest of her plan into action. "Brother," she said. "I don't really know much about building, but I think I am making faster progress than you because you spend so much time quarreling with your workers. Let me give you this string of little bells. You can tie them around your waist so your men can hear you and work faster when they hear you approach. That way you can save a lot of time that's now being lost."

The brother liked the idea and hung the bells around his waist. From then on, every time he arrived on the work site he found to his delight that they were working hard. This pleased him so much that he started complimenting them. It soon became a habit for him to cheer his workers on and regularly spend extra time each day honoring the men who were building the great church. He even became popular with his working crew. His men pushed themselves with a new sense of personal pride and urgency and gradually they caught up and passed the workforce laboring on the other half of the church. The brother won the contest.

Years after the church was finished the sister admitted to her brother that the sole goal of the contest had been to cure him of his offensive and overbearing disposition. She feared he would be angry but instead he was thankful for the lesson he had learned. So thankful, in fact, that after hearing her story he commissioned a statue of himself wearing the bells around his waist and had it set up in front of the church to remind him and every person like him who saw the statue that real power comes from approaching men and God with thankfulness and gratitude. Power does not come from telling, pushing, or shouting. The sister could have told her brother how he needed to change, but she didn't. She found a way for him to discover how he should change on his own. He discovered that people work much harder when they respect their leader and the goals they are working towards. The man also learned that it feels great to be well-liked by the people working for him. He learned the great lesson taught by Christ, "We love him because he first loved us."[2]

---

2.   *1 John 4:19*

Chapter ELEVEN

CONSIDER A KIND QUESTION

Leadership is based on inspiration not domination; on cooperation, not intimidation.

William Arthur Wood

One of the first lessons a person learns in business is that the best way to get someone else to do something is to make that person think it is his own idea. This works in parenting and education, too. As teachers, we find the hardest part of the job is figuring out how to help people discover what we already know. It is tempting just to stand up and tell everyone what is right and wrong and then go home, but that method doesn't reach many people. It has a way of bouncing off the forehead of some and going in one ear and out the other of others. In business schools we often use case studies that challenge students to identify an issue, and then we encourage them to identify, explore and debate the various solutions until they individually uncover the learning points. The process takes patience and can be painful, but if it's done well the students become involved and are able to internalize the lessons we're trying to teach them. Teaching a case study requires that we ask questions instead of just giving out answers.

"What the boss asked me was really more of a 'kind question.' He just wanted to know how soon I could clean out my desk and be off company property."

A good manager is a busy person. Such people have agendas and are eager to move those agendas forward. They are under pressure to produce quick results. It is understandable that the thought of patiently asking questions rather than telling people what to do never occurs to some managers. On the other hand, a good manager understands the huge difference between "efficiency" and "effectiveness." Telling people what to do is efficient, but not necessarily effective. Asking questions to bring employees in line with a manager's plan takes a little more time and thoughtful preparation, but the results are usually worth that extra effort.

What is a kind question?

Not all questions are kind questions. Once, in an interview, an employee told us about a call she received from her manager. He immediately asked, "When will you be getting me those training materials I asked for?" His manner was abrupt, and this was not a kind question, particularly since she had hand-delivered the documents to her manager several weeks earlier. It would have been easy for the employee to react with anger, but she didn't. Like many other employees in today's work environment, she takes thoughtlessness and meanness for granted among people in managerial positions. What could her manager have said when she answered his phone call? Possibly he could have started by saying, "I've looked around here in the office but I can't find the training materials that we'll be using next week. Am I right in thinking that you already dropped them off here?" That is a kind question. It addresses the problem, shares the responsibility and still gets to the point.

A chemical waste manager once described the long history of chemists at his organization who weren't filling out their waste log sheets. Sounds like a simple problem, but in order to safely dispose of the waste containers, his workers must know what's in them. The manager provides laboratories with containers and log sheets, but most researchers won't fill in the log sheets until the container is full. By then, the researchers often can't remember which chemicals went into each container. In fact, sometimes his staff goes out to pick up a full container and the log sheet is still completely blank, so they must leave the container. Of course, this is frustrating for the chemists and for his staff and causes extra work and wasted time.

The first impulse that hit the manager was to send out reminder emails to all the laboratories. But that hadn't worked in the past, so out of desperation the manager tried something a little different. He

Ask for Help
Learn to ask for help rather than react with anger when you believe someone is letting you down. It is a kind question.

decided instead to send an email asking the chemists for their ideas about keeping track of the potentially dangerous contents of the chemical waste containers. He clearly listed the objectives of the waste-disposal program, the safety issues involved, added the ideas that had been considered in the past, and then he waited for their replies. Three things happened. First, more of the log sheets started being filled out by the chemists. Second, he received several good suggestions that would make log sheets more accurate. And equally important, the chemists started showing greater appreciation for the chemical waste manager, his staff and the service they provided.

Asking for help is a kind question. Val Christensen, a negotiations instructor at the Marriott School of Management, puts it this way: "When you find yourself negotiating in a tight spot, try asking the other side for help. Most people are genuinely good and caring people. If we sincerely ask for help, they will be more willing to listen to our side of the argument and offer ideas without attacking us." This is wise counsel. In many ways, business leadership of the best kind is basically a series of thoughtful negotiations between managers and employees.

Chapter TWELVE

CARROT IS BETTER THAN STICK

> *You do not lead by hitting people over the head; that's assault, not leadership.*
>
> Dwight D. Eisenhower

Behavioral psychologists tell us that there are four ways to motivate good behavior and/or stop bad behavior. The methods are called negative reinforcement, punishment, extinction, and positive reinforcement. Negative reinforcement is used by leaders to make employees miserable until the employees do what the leaders demand. Nagging and making threats are widely-used tactics for applying negative reinforcement. Punishment is self-explanatory. When someone does a bad thing, the leader hits them over the head. That's the way many armies have operated throughout history, but it's still " . . . assault, not leadership." Like punish-

The carrot or the stick?

ment, extinction is aimed at stopping bad behavior. The idea is to take away the pleasure associated with doing a "bad" thing. For example, extinction is used to help people quit smoking cigarettes by slowly reducing the amount of nicotine contained in the cigarette or even giving a strong electrical shock each time a person takes a puff. Positive reinforcement is the only carrot in the group of behavioral methods . . . rewarding people for doing good things.

The trouble is, however, that rewarding people for doing good things apparently goes against the natural inclinations of leaders. Motivational researcher Claude Steiner[3] observes that as children we learn from our parents that people (a) don't reward even when they have rewards to give, (b) don't ask for rewards when they need them, (c) don't accept rewards when they need them, (d) don't reject rewards even when they don't want them, and (e) don't give themselves the rewards they really want.

Rewarding people for doing good things, despite human nature, is nonetheless effective.[4] Leaders don't need to psychoanalyze employees and uncover why they do what they do. They only need to find out what they like and give it to them when they perform well.

Stick: The apparent tool of choice

When it comes to leaders finding ways to shape the behavior of those under them, a big hard stick outnumbers a juicy orange carrot three-to-one. Unfortunately, the stick is impressive but it causes resentment. It activates the Hate Group and sows the seeds of underperformance, passive-aggressiveness, burnout and turnover. For anyone who feels stick management is not a problem, consider this statistic: 25% of American workers recently polled admit they are showing up at work just to collect a paycheck.[5] Perhaps the attitude is best expressed by a group of USAF reservists we talked to in upstate New York. We wanted to explore several key dimensions of loyalty and patriotism among men and women serving in the Armed Forces

---

3.   *Scripts People Live* by Claude M. Steiner
4.   *1001 Ways to Rewards Employees* by Bob Nelson
5.   *TNS* for the Conference Board

Reserve. We asked the reservists to give us some reasons they decided to continue serving after spending twenty years on active duty. The unanimous reply surprised us—"the Air Force spent twenty-years sticking it to us. Now we are going to stick it to the Air Force."

The stick, it is argued in its defense, gives managers short-term gains. In the long run, however, the stick is destructive to workplace morale and it is sure to cause resentment, slowdowns and very possibly loss of the best workers. Using the stick makes managers look cruel, weak, and just plain foolish, particularly in the eyes of our new generation of workers. In our management research and consulting work, we have found that in every organization that uses the stick method of leadership, stick leadership causes identifiable bitterness and drains employee energy.

The stick method causes a highly productive employee to lose an annual bonus because he was seen playing solitaire on company time. An administrator using the stick method threatened to take away the annual raise of an employee for not completing a personal productivity report, when the report had actually been completed months earlier but lost by the records department. In some businesses we even find the archetypal Ebenezer Scrooge who relentlessly works all through the day from early morning to late in the evening (having food brought into them at lunchtime) expecting everyone else to do the same, and questioning the loyalty of those who do not. If you were the employee in any of those situations, how would you feel about going the extra mile for your employer a month later when the company's survival depends on your help? How many extra hours would you work? (And that question, by the way, is an example of teaching by asking kind questions. It didn't hurt, did it?)

The discipline of carrot

Learning to reward may require a lot of retraining on the part of the manager as well as the employee. Because leadership by stick is all too common among families, we may have to unlearn what we learned as children. The ultimate goal is to reverse the attitudes about rewards which we've already seen outlined above by Professor Steiner.

Leaders should give rewards when they have them to give. Employees should ask for rewards when they want them. Employees should accept rewards if they want them. Employees should reject manipulative rewards. And we all should give ourselves rewards.

When we can turn to our newspaper's police news to find out what's happening in some of our nation's largest and most influential corporations, it's a signal to us that it may be hard in today's business climate to cultivate a discipline of carrot instead of stick. When corporate leaders take millions of dollars in annual bonuses, even the newest employees know that there are generous rewards available for employees that are not being offered or given. Employees are cleverly encouraged not to ask for raises or other rewards. Managers establish supposedly "ethical" rules and policies that discourage employees from discussing salaries. Obviously, this is done to reinforce the employee taboo of reward-asking. Employees learn to be defensive and deflect rather than embrace compliments from managers. Co-workers often scorn "employees of the month" or anyone else accepting recognition awards, deeming them to be "brown noses." Employees begrudgingly shape their on-the-job behavior and compromise personal standards just to receive financial incentive rewards. And too many of us, as frontline managers, consistently deny ourselves rewards we feel we have earned for fear of appearing selfish. The image comes to mind of crabs pulling each other down as they attempt to climb out of a bucket.

Leaders who understand the power of people working together harmoniously with a common, acceptable goal in mind, and who are willing to make the effort, have the power to build a discipline of carrot in their organizations. Seven-time Tour de France champion Lance Armstrong knows how to reward and keep his team positive. His long-time coach Chris Carmichael says it would be easy for Lance's teammates to hold back in reserve one percent of their effort just in case they had a chance to win a stage of the race for themselves. But they don't because he generously shares the increased rewards they achieve through teamwork.

Chapter THIRTEEN

Make the Journey Using Switchbacks & Stepping Stones

No man will make a great leader who wants to do it all himself, or to get all the credit for doing it.

Andrew Carnegie

The mountains surround us where we live. One mountain just northeast of our neighborhood rises to nearly 12,000 feet. One of the fun summer activities for teenagers in the local area is to climb several thousand feet to the top of this mountain and then slide down the icy glacier on its eastern face. Some people make it up and down in one day. Others stay the night on the mountain top, then slide down the following day. Some people never make it at all. There are two ways to climb this mountain. There are a few climbers who blaze a trail straight up the mountain. But most people prefer to walk a well-worn path to the top which is filled with switchbacks and stepping stones. Climbers blazing a trail go alone. Perhaps they are loners or just impatient. In the end, they want to get to the top as fast as they can so that they can slide down the glacier. If others don't get there as fast, well, that's not their problem. Climbers following the switchbacks often travel in large groups. For them most of the fun in making the climb and sliding down the glacier comes when the whole group can slide down together.

Just as there are two ways to climb that mountain, there are two ways for a leader to accomplish a task. Many leaders only know about the direct route. They are familiar with the task and know the path needed to accomplish it. They may have traveled the path so many times that now they even feel bored with the climb. And with the pressure to perform and move on to the next task, they don't want to waste time climbing a well-known peak. They may say to themselves, "If some of the people don't get there or don't enjoy the climb, well, that is their loss." Perhaps this is why many leaders are stuck in the sad situation of getting things done on their own, with little or no support. We believe leaders should find ways to use, figuratively speaking, as many switchbacks and stepping stones as necessary so that 100% of their group can get to the top of the mountain. We know leaders who are willing to sacrifice some detail and some personal goals in order to build energy and appreciation for the journey. They have faith that people who learn to love a task will keep working at the task until it is mastered.

Advantages and disadvantages of switchbacks

Using these "workplace switchbacks" gives everyone a chance to stop, catch their breath, refresh their energy and ultimately enjoy a new, broader, and grander point of view about themselves and what they are doing. Planning short-term switchbacks for current projects, and planning ahead for long-term career switchbacks, however,

It Matters How You Climb the Mountain

	Direct Route	Using Switchbacks
Advantages	1. Quicker to climb to the top. 2. Less day-to-day thinking. Just outline the task and/or details and move on. 3. Able to cover a lot of ground.	1. Most people will make it to the top. 2. Inspires more love for the cause and the leader. 3. People develop better skills and gain commitment. 4. Everyone has fun and share positive experiences.
Disadvantages	1. Few make it to the top. 2. Need to push or even carry people to attain goals. 3. Most people will resent the cause, the leader and/or the goals.	1. Requires more creative thinking and planning. 2. Must identify and give extra help to stragglers. 3. Takes more time to reach the top.

puts enormous responsibilities on the shoulders of the leaders. They must start thinking about much more than just what task they want performed and what guidelines and/or outcomes they want to drive home. They must plan the types of activities, questions and feedback that will engage the group over the long haul. People need to discover the beauty of the path they are following. Plus-One leaders know that the quality and enjoyment of the climb to the top is critically important to attaining meaningful goals. How we deliver our leadership message is at least as important as the message itself.

A friend once shocked a roomful of professors by saying, "What value is it to our students when we cover a half dozen topics in a single class if they can only master about a dozen in the whole course?" "I'd rather cover ten topics in the course well enough so that every student can master all ten. If the best students are interested in the topic, they can always take another course to learn more." He added that, "I find it odd that so many of us spend all our time and energy racing to cover an entire textbook of information in a single course rather than spending most of our time figuring out how to make concepts real and memorable." He tied it all up by saying, "If the activities are engaging, if the accomplishments are recognized, if the value of the material is demonstrated, then students will connect with the subject matter. If the end of the term comes too soon to satisfy their curiosity, well, when there is a love of learning, learning never has to stop." Of course, the same can be said for employees and their day-to-day work responsibilities.

Every time managers take time to play a game, recognize an accomplishment, or just genuinely listen, they are getting off the direct path and helping employees enjoy a switchback. For example, a local software company was feverishly working to meet a new product-release deadline. Because of the time crunch, engineers were working six and seven days a week and putting in many more hours than they normally did.

One of the managers happened to pass one of the work-stressed engineers in a company hallway and stopped to ask how he was doing. The engineer described how hard it was to work sixty-hour weeks. Even though the manager had worked sixty-hour weeks throughout his own career, he smiled and said, "Well, you do look a bit tired." The engineer then frowned and responded, "Yeah, and this is all your fault." The manager decided it was time for a switchback, so he chuckled as he asked, "What do you mean, my fault?" The engineer's frown disappeared and he grinned as he admitted, "Well, we have to blame someone!" The manager replied, "I'll gladly take the blame then. But thank you for working those long hours and keep it up. It's good for you and it's going to be good for all of us." The engineer laughed, waved and continued down the hallway.

That manager just needed to give the engineer time to pause for a few minutes to harmlessly let off some steam and refresh his energy. What could have turned into an ugly and unnecessary confrontation ended up pulling manager and employee closer together in a common cause. Switchbacks don't need to be complicated in order to be effective.

Stepping stones build momentum

As we climb up the mountain that leads to our ultimate goal we want to take some stops along the way to rest, appreciate the beauty of what has been obtained, and celebrate the good choices and hard work that have brought us to where we are. As managers, we can help employees do this by placing stepping stones on their path to success and provide opportunities for celebration. The value of celebrating the moment seems obvious, yet we've observed very few organizations that recognize its importance or do it well, consistently.

Several years ago, we conducted a round of personal interviews in the customer service department of a leading credit card company. The company was trying to find ways to improve employee productivity. As we walked around the department with the management team we noticed lots of shiny stars and confetti covering some of the work area carpets. When we asked about them, the management team frowned and then groused about the problem of team leaders throwing impromptu parties to celebrate individual and team achievements. Managers said that they felt the celebrations were hurting productivity and that work rules were in place to discourage the practice. We thought the managers had an odd point of view, so later, during the personal interviews, we asked employees about the impromptu parties. They said they loved to celebrate accomplishments, but that management was changing the time-based account-

Don't be afraid to let your team celebrate!
Build momentum in your team by having consistent celebrations along the way.

ability and productivity rules, which was making it harder to have these parties.

The company's productivity problems no longer surprised us. The productivity of frontline employees usually revolves around the quality of the supervisor. From an employee's point of view, good supervisors stand out because of the emotional support they provide; bad supervisors stand out because of their insensitivity to employee needs, concerns, and accomplishments. From a management point of view, good supervisors stand out because of their ability to meet productivity goals; bad supervisors stand out because of their insensitivity to company rules and policies. Consequently, management is always surprised by the real, measurable impact that supportive and sensitive supervisors have on the confidence and productivity of frontline workers. While managers understand the positive impact of a good supervisor, they don't realize that a good supervisor needs to find fun ways to celebrate day-to-day accomplishments. To encourage employees, they need stepping stones. The shiny stars and confetti were the only signs of hope and encouragement we observed on that trip. We begged the company managers not to remove those colorful "stepping stones."

Creating your own stepping stones

We attended a marketing seminar in which the consultant was trying to inject some new energy into a sluggish business. At the end of the day, he had us participate in what he called a "consumer marketing theater." He divided the group into three teams and assigned each team to act out how consumers might react to a shopping experience in their warehouse-style grocery store if it were filmed either as (1) an action-adventure movie, (2) a romantic comedy, or (3) a thriller-horror movie.

The teams had about twenty minutes to improvise a story complete with actors, script, sound effects, and props. As the teams performed their "movie," the rest of the group laughed and encouraged their coworkers. After the teams presented, the group voted with applause for their favorite presentation. The consultant then asked

"They weren't supposed to be literal!"

the groups to vote on gag prizes for "biggest ham," "least likely to have a successful acting career," etc. In this exercise everyone felt like a star. To top off the session, the consultant made two big columns on a blackboard and took notes as the teams outlined what they tried to show him about the consumer's shopping experience in their skit and the suggestions they would have for their store.

After summarizing all the contributions, the consultant then told about a three-year research study sponsored by a large retailing association. It turned out the three groups made similar observations and recommendations as the expensive research study, but more precisely attuned to the context of their specific business. After agreeing on some action items, the consultant closed the session by congratulating the teams for making the exercise fun and for doing such a good job applying what they learned.

According to the consultant, year after year that simple, almost out-of-control exercise is a turning point for many businesses. The evaluation forms collected after the seminar frequently highlight the "theater" by saying "the experience helped me put everything together that we'd been doing throughout the day," "a fun activity that made me feel that I could apply what I learned," "gave me a way to look at our marketing through new eyes," and so on. We feel that it works because it is a fun way for people to celebrate the performance of the teams in creating the skits as well as in applying and tying together many of that day's learning points. The consultant heightens the whole experience by pausing long enough to recognize what specific individuals and the group as a whole have accomplished. He builds energy by creating stepping stones for the organization.

Too often in life we quickly gloss over accomplishments and good choices people are making just to put a spotlight on problems or shortcomings. We look backward with resentment rather than forward with excitement. This is particularly true in our everyday working world. There are a lot of different "hats" each of us can wear as we go through life. At times we should remember to wear our "curious hat." At other times our hat of choice should be emotional, organized, creative, cheerful, and sometimes, when it is warranted, even critical.

In fact, it is unproductive for a manager to wear only one hat all the time. We all want to be tough, no-nonsense professionals, but every now and then it is good for our own benefit, as well as of even greater benefits to the people we lead, to take off our "critical hat," put on our "cheerful hat" and celebrate the victories along the way. Identifying the stepping stones that led to success and celebrating that success often provides a workforce with the internal momentum to get "ordinary people" to accomplish extraordinary things.

Part THREE

Creating a Learning Atmosphere

Part THREE

CREATING A LEARNING ATMOSPHERE

A "learning organization" is defined by Peter Senge[1] as an organization "where people continually expand their capacity to create the results they truly desire, where new and expansive patterns of thinking are nurtured, where collective aspiration is set free, and where people are continually learning to see the whole together." Now, who wouldn't want all that?

While Art Kliener[2] was developing *The Fifth Disciple Fieldbook*, he came up with several reasons why a manager should encourage and enable a learning organization within his or her own office structure. Among the positive results of such an organization he identified:

- Superior performance and competitive advantage

- Better customer relations

- Avoiding decline

- Improvement of quality

- Encouragement of innovation

- Improvement of spiritual and personal well being

- An increase of individuals' abilities to manage change because the times we live in demand it

---

1. *The Fifth Discipline* by Peter Senge

2. *Fifth Discipline Fieldbook* by Peter Senge and Art Kleiner

One manager writes: "I want learning organizations primarily because I think they provide the healthiest kind of environment for human beings to be in. I am only secondarily interested in the bottom line efficiency of organizations, and I feel that maximum effectiveness is achieved through continuous learning resulting in continuous improvement. I personally am interested in helping people explore alternatives in their own lives, both personal and professional, and want to take responsibility for bringing their vision of *better* into reality."

The concept of a learning organization is compelling, but before a learning organization can function the manager must first cultivate a "learning atmosphere" among the people she works with and directs. Without a learning atmosphere functioning smoothly in the day-to-day work environment, the corporate goal of an effective learning organization is little more than a joke. Not long ago, when we telephoned a former client, she sarcastically greeted us with, "This is the Corporate Strategy and Plans Department, getting smarter and continually improving every day in every way!" She was obviously not truly enthusiastic about the way a learning-organization strategy was being implemented in her office, because employees are rightly skeptical of all the talk about learning organizations, if they haven't yet experienced a learning atmosphere.

Learning atmosphere defined

A learning atmosphere is one in which (1) everyone gets to express their honest thoughts and feelings, (2) everyone listens respectfully and attentively, and (3) everyone feels a sense of camaraderie and shares a bond of friendship. Sounds good! Intuitively, however, we tend to be a little afraid of honest thoughts and feelings in an office setting, even among people we like and trust. We are afraid to express ourselves entirely honestly because—in addition to simply not wanting to hurt anyone's feelings—we may offend someone who has the power either to hurt us or perhaps stop helping us. We are afraid to listen to other's expressed frankness because those expressions may be negative in some way about us, personally,

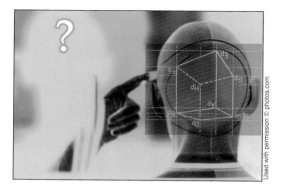

Learning Organizations
Energize your organization by cultivating a learning atmosphere.

and we don't really want to change. But if we can somehow express ourselves candidly, not be threatening and take care to avoid hurtful statements, then we are making real progress for building a learning atmosphere.

Once getting past the first requirement of a learning atmosphere, the second requirement in our list of three criteria may also give us trouble. Listening respectfully and attentively simply goes against force of habit. Simply said, people tend to criticize or ignore opinions that don't mesh with their own predetermined ideas of how to do the work. Finally, if managers, dynamic or not, recklessly put into practice the first and second criteria of a learning atmosphere, it is almost guaranteed that they will seriously damage existing office camaraderie and established friendships. Managers who have seen such calamities happen, and possibly have even been responsible, call this "Being OB'd." This is a term and an abbreviation identifying a group whose morale, effectiveness, productivity and sometimes even interpersonal relationships have been seriously hammered by organizational behaviorists who treat an office organization as a laboratory experiment instead of people with individual talents, skills, and personalities.

Proceed with caution or get OB'd

We always sit down with managers before starting any corporate training program to discuss the organization's program goals, the schedule, and the training materials. Even when the training topic is marketing, managers sometimes get a concerned look in their eyes. They ask us, "You're not going to OB my organization, are you?" When we first heard that term, we didn't understand what it meant so we asked if being OB'd is a good thing or a bad thing. They explained that it is a bad thing that hurts productivity and camaraderie. They said that in their experience, an OB'd business can take up to a year or more to recover. We certainly didn't want to do that, so we asked, "What happens when someone OB's an organization?" "Well," they began, "It's when a group of organizational behavior consultants come in and elicit the frank and honest opinions, that is, criticisms from all the employees, spread their findings throughout the organization, and consequently destroy the organization from within... it's like that Trojan Horse in Greek legend!"

Letting everyone in an organization fully express themselves is a worthy goal, but it is also a risky operation. It can and must be done, but not without sufficient training in the use of some pretty powerful leadership tools. The next five chapters describe some of the most potent strategies and tactics we use consistently in our business-leadership work. We learned some of these concepts from very successful leaders and discovered others for ourselves. We use these tactics to enhance and sometimes even restructure working environments of companies to build effective learning organizations that are management-friendly, employee-friendly, and meet the specific goals of those client companies. These skills have changed our lives and we have seen them change the lives of many others. Thoughtfully applied, they will not OB an organization or sink an individual manager's career, but will significantly elevate both.

Chapter FOURTEEN

Cultivate a Believing Mindset

Human beings, by changing the inner attitudes of their minds, can change the outer aspects of their lives.

William James

If you want to successfully manage people, then you must first manage your mindset. We can know all the right principles and use all the right tactics, but we may still be ineffective leaders because of the way we think about the people we lead. People rarely stop and think about their mindset, because it's just part of an individual's personality, and it's sometimes jealously protected by the individual because it's what sets that person apart from everyone else. On the other hand, sometimes the individual's mindset, however it sets that person apart, can be destructive to that individual's efforts to become a dynamic and effective leader of others. We can immediately start being better leaders by realizing that, and by making some adjustments to the lens through which we view others.

Your mindset determines how much power you really have to influence others. Having the wrong mindset will only hamper, possibly even derail your success as a leader. This is critical, so we'll say it again. We have found time and time again that an individual who combines our leadership tactics with a wrong mindset will almost always achieve only mediocre results and sometimes completely fail as a leader.

The believing mindset

I like you. I think you are interesting, and I want to get to know you. I believe you are capable of doing great things.

These phrases are in boldface because they're important. Write them down on a poster and tack it to a wall where you'll see it frequently. Remind yourself of it every day. These three simple sentence embody the "believing mindset." It is an inner attitude about people that has the power to change almost everything about your life.

"You like me. You really like me," gushed the TV actress turned film star as she accepted an Academy Award for being named the best actress of the year. For her, the award was spectacular confirmation that she was well liked and respected within an extremely competitive, close-knit community. We all like to be liked. Knowing that we are liked, or appreciated, or needed, is wonderful, because it fills us with energy and the determination to keep on improving. When we learn how to give others this feeling, it is simply amazing how well so many things turn out for us. However, for some people, developing a believing mindset is elusive. We have observed many leaders who seem to be thinking, "I distrust you, don't want to know you, and don't believe you are capable of doing much of anything."

For example, this advice has been given by sage-like academics to young professors at universities for decades: "You can either lead the stars or walk the dogs." The implication here is that one should focus on nurturing "stars" and leave the "dogs" to fight for the scraps that fall beneath the table. By now, everyone hoping to become effective in managing people should realize that they are headed for serious trouble if they start seeing people only in terms of "stars" and "dogs." The truth is, everyone is a potential star. Everyone of us has a touch of the extraordinary inside of him or her. All too often we let our attitudes, our preconceptions, our flawed mindsets, get in the way. When this happens we find, often too late and always to our great disappointment, that our own success, even more than the success of those we are trying to manage, is limited more by our own attitude about others than by innate ability. Learn that early and never forget it.

Oops! My negative mindset is showing

A memorable scene from the movie, *The Paper Chase*, shows the renowned, inscrutable law school professor, Dr. Kingsfield, calling a student down to the front of the classroom after he finds that the young man is unprepared to answer one of his questions. Kingsfield pulls a coin from his pocket and says, "Mr. Hart, here is a dime. Call your mother. Tell her there is serious doubt about your becoming a lawyer."

On the surface this seems like cruel and embarrassing treatment and indeed, Professor Kingsfield did humiliate the unprepared student. He singled him out to make everyone in the class fearful of being unprepared. However, as the movie so clearly shows, the brilliant Prof. Kingsfield's fatal weakness was not his behavior towards that one unfortunate student. Embarrassing him with a little joke was harmless enough. In fact, the whole routine might be fun and help break the tension and monotony of a long and difficult class. We find fault with Prof. Kingsfield's mindset. His contemptuous attitude towards his suffering students is a key element in the movie and overshadows everything else he does. Everyone knows he doesn't care about the students. All of his students feel that they can never measure up to his impossible standard.

To Kingsfield, people are nameless and faceless except for their blurred, black and white pictures on his seating chart. He walks by them in the hallway without acknowledging them. He calls on people to respond to questions without even realizing the students are not in class that day. Even at the end of the year, when most teachers can recall student names, a student tells the professor, "You really mean something to me and your class has really meant something to me." Kingsfield stares blankly at the student and unemotionally asks, "What was your name?" The end result is, when the final grades come out, that same student folds his unopened grade report into a paper airplane and tosses it into the ocean.

It is a defining moment. The teacher and the university have lost their power to influence—to lead. If the student is not important to the professor, then what the professor has to say is important to the student only to the point of meeting established course requirements. As the saying goes, "I don't care what you know until I know how much you care." Indifference is returned with indifference. Contempt is returned with contempt. In every walk of life, whether it is education, business or some other social situation, every individual is a powerful mirror.

Most managers don't plan on offending their employees. Perhaps they just forget other people also have feelings. We once attended a retirement luncheon in which several of our colleagues were recognized for their many decades of service and contribution to the university. First, the speakers failed to recognize and include two of our colleagues attending the luncheon who had just retired the previous year without any special fanfare. Second, they presented rocking chairs to the current set of retirees. One can imagine how both groups of retirees could have been offended, respectively, by the snub and by the somewhat tasteless joke that the retirees were of no more use. The first group might leave the luncheon feeling unappreciated and unvalued. After all, why didn't anyone make a fuss over them when they retired? The second group might leave the luncheon feeling insulted. Do the administrators believe we are so old, helpless and useless that all we are good for is sitting by a fire in a rocking chair?

In another famous film, *My Fair Lady*, the fine music and story of a self-centered British elocution expert and his unfortunate student eloquently emphasize an important life lesson about the dan-

My Fair Lady © Warner Brothers Pictures

Let your stars shine!
Every person has a star inside ready to shine. Have the courage and patience to bring out the star in everyone.

ger of having a very negative mindset. Observing the rudeness with which the snobbish Professor Higgins is treating poor flower-seller Eliza Dolittle, Higgins' friend, Colonel Pickering asks with alarm, "Does it occur to you, Higgins, that the girl has some feelings?" Prof. Higgins replies, "Oh no, I don't think so. No feelings we'd worry about." "She should be grateful," Higgins says. "I'll make a queen of that barbarous wretch."

What should leaders who see this film be thinking? It's simple. People want to know their leaders like them and have confidence in them. They want to be treated like a friend, not like a child, subordinate, or easily dismissed servant. A Plus-One leader always considers people—individuals working in his or her group—to be more important than keeping up with a project schedule or immediately meeting a company goal. Such leaders know that if they take care of the individuals working with them in the short term, in the long term those people—all individuals—will respond, take care of the business, and come through to meet tight deadlines.

During one consulting experience, working again with the customer service organization of a large credit card company, we conducted one of the more memorable personal interviews we have ever experienced. We were talking with an employee who had been flagged by the company as being a poor performer. She impressed us as being bright and cheerful. As we reviewed some of her negative experiences she remembered from work, she mentioned an occasion when her supervisor was watching over her shoulder as she handled a customer complaint. She explained:

> "I still remember like it was yesterday. I was talking
> with a customer and did something the supervisor

disagreed with. He looked down at me and said why are you doing it this way? Didn't you read your email?"

We then asked her, "When he said that, what do you think he was he thinking about you?" Unable to fight back the tears, she said, "He was thinking that I'm an idiot . . . that I'm not capable of doing the job right." After listening to this young woman, we realized how difficult it must be for a person to become a top performer when their manager's attitude makes them feel like a fool. People know how we feel about them even when we don't say it directly. And how people feel about themselves is strongly influenced by what they believe other people are thinking about them.

The absent mindset

Many ineffective leaders don't monitor the attitude they project towards others. They have an absent mindset. They let the emotion of the moment manage their mindset. If they are happy, then everyone is happy, doing great, meeting all expectations! If the leader is unhappy, embarrassed, stressed out, feeling any negative emotion, then everyone is useless, plotting, even sinister. Perhaps you have witnessed in someone an acute case of negativism brought on by an absent mindset. An absent mindset, just like an acute attack of some physical illness, can inflict long lasting damage and suffering. The measure of a great manager is the ability to keep sending out positive vibrations, regardless of the traffic ticket they got driving in to work that morning, and the toothache that kicked in right after the paper cut.

The Plus-One mindset

Plus-One leaders are always asking themselves three questions:

1. Does everyone know that I like them?

2. Does everyone know how interested I am in them?

    3. Does everyone know how much confidence I have in their abilities?

No matter what the circumstances, or the pressure, or the tiredness, a good manager tries very, very hard not to react mindlessly to what a person may thoughtlessly say. A manager must vigilantly try not to appear frustrated, angry, or say things that will later be regretted.

Rather, we learned long ago that we can manage our mindset and keep it on the positive track by playing the game "Red? Yellow? Green?" That is, mentally categorizing comments as coming from the Hate Group, Swing Group, or Love Group. Once we identify the type of individual in front of us, we know a lot about how to manage the relationship. We know the correct color of tactic to apply. If a comment comes from the Hate Group, think of the red survival tactics discussed in Part One of this book. The tactics protect us from the bad things that can happen out there when the Hate Group snaps into action. Get out the Garbage helps us identify the Hate Group and Be like Columbo ensures that we will be an elusive target for irresponsible criticism. Whereas, Pai Ma Pi and Play it, Don't Say it enable us to keep doing our job and focusing on results until we can gain employee support and identify strong allies. There is no tact without tactics and cultivating a believing mindset gives tactics their power.

Chapter FIFTEEN

EMPLOYEES SAY THE DARNDEST THINGS!

Tact is the knack of making a point without making an enemy.

Sir Isaac Newton

Learning organizations are designed to give everybody the opportunity, the forum and the confidence to have their say, but managers, regardless of their best efforts in every area of good management, should be ready for what they are likely to hear. One way to think about the comments people come up with is to arrange the spectrum of possibilities into a scale ranging from the reddest, most negative comments, i.e., the personal attack, to the greenest, most positive comments, i.e., the love note. Each type of comment presents us with challenges to recognize it for what it is and respond to it powerfully and with an eye to the long-term effect of the words that come out of our mouths and expressions that come out on our faces.

PERSONAL ATTACK	NEGATIVE SPIN	OUTRAGEOUS OUTBURST	NON SEQUITUR	LOVE NOTE

Personal attack in sheep's clothing

We have read that 90% of questions managers get asked are direct or indirect personal attacks. That unpleasant statistic may be right, but we believe that the seriousness of the "attack" element in the stated question ultimately depends on who the question comes from. We certainly need to be particularly careful when responding to questions from the Hate Group. A direct attack from the Hate Group is only one way people try to undermine leadership.

There are many indirect passive-aggressive attacks, all of which mean pretty much the same thing: "Hey, stupid! You're doing it the wrong way!"

There is the confrontational question: "Why would you do it that way?" We hear this one around the house quite a lot. There is the "dueling expert" question: "Well, I wouldn't do it that way." The "country dumb" question: "Golly gee. I haven't worked in a big corporation before. Do you think you could explain why we are doing it this way?"

Of course, active non-participation is also a negative tactic. It expresses itself through back row mumbling, newspaper reading, MP3s, PDAs, text messaging, instant messaging, surfing the internet with laptops, etc. And of course, backhanded compliments are sometimes tossed out unexpectedly: "That is really good work for someone with your level of experience."

Why non sequiturs shouldn't bother us

A non sequitur is defined as a statement that does not follow logically from what preceded it. We have all heard them, coming at us often right when we think we are one with our team and finally getting to the key points of our presentation. Such statements may bother

us, may even throw us off balance, but they shouldn't. At worst, a non sequitur is just a juvenile ploy to gain attention or—better, but still unsettling—perhaps just a bored participant's effort to move a tedious discussion in a more positive direction. In which case it is something similar to an outrageous outburst.

Consider a friendly gathering in someone's home, and somehow the discussion evolves into a humorous disagreement about the origin of the common chicken. Freddie says, "I think the chicken came first, and started laying eggs to produce other chickens." Mabel says, "No. The egg came first, and from that all chickens evolved." Al, wanting to be part of this highly intellectual conversation, pipes up, "I think the omelette came first." His non sequitur, while vaguely related to the conversation already in progress, effectively silences both Mabel and Fred, who mentally make a note to themselves never to invite Al over again.

Most of the time, though, a non sequitur originates with an interested and thoughtful person who desperately wants to contribute but is having a hard time connecting with the topic. A non sequitur raises a red flag. Often it signals that a leader is having a hard time getting to the "what, so what, and now what" of the meeting's main issue. A non sequitur, while it may stop us in our tracks while we try to digest it and connect it to what is being discussed, doesn't really tell us anything too negative about a person's attitude.

Clueless about love

We want to believe that everyone recognizes encouragement when they hear it, but there are several types of love notes that may be ignored or unfortunately cause some defensiveness. One manager wrote about an experience in which she was presenting a new incentive plan to a room full of salespeople. She was well prepared and confidently moved through her material. However, as she was finishing up the meeting, several salespeople spoke up, starting to attack several parts of her plan. Before she could reply, one of the other

salespeople spoke up to defend the plan. Even though she did not realize it at the time, that sudden and spirited defense of her plan is a love note and it shouldn't be ignored, because management needs all the capable allies it can get to reach its short-term and long-term goals.

Another manager in a customer service center described to us the frustration he feels when customer service representatives suggest changes to the company's standard operating procedures. The manager admitted that usually these employees are very productive and competent, but he can't help but feel annoyed that the employees won't leave well enough alone. He feels, "If it ain't broke don't fix it." Good employees know they are taking a risk when suggesting changes, but they do it because they believe the manager likes and respects them and that the manager knows that, in turn, they like and respect the manager. When a good employee makes a suggestion, it is a love note. Alas, this love usually is unrequited, and the employee's positive reinforcement of managerial plans and procedures ends up being dampened and forgotten.

Bottom line, once employees start talking openly to managers much of what they say is negative or can be interpreted as negative. The challenge for the leader is to not make the situation worse (and start down a leadership death spiral) by reacting badly to the negativity. The next chapters share ideas for dealing with every type of comment with confidence and positivism!

Chapter SIXTEEN

MANAGERS SEE IT LIKE...EMPLOYEES SEE IT LIKE...

P eople are a bundle of emotions. We all like to think that we are logical and level-headed in all our dealings, but there is a preponderance of evidence that shows we simply are not. There are numerous stories that point out this human frailty. For example, you may have heard the anecdote about the time when a manager accidentally knocked an item off an employee's desk. The employee slowly got up, walked over to the manager's desk and swept every item on the desk onto the floor while muttering, "I'll show that manager for disrespecting me!".

Or consider the sad, but true, time when a restaurant manager became annoyed with a new employee for asking too many questions. Wordlessly, the fed-up manager hosed him down with hot oil from the deep fryers. Definitely not the

This probably isn't a good time to ask him how often we're supposed to change the cooking oil.

© BYU Academic Publishing

sort of act that builds employee confidence or good teamwork. Or, how about the time when an AOL customer service representative got so upset and angry about a long and difficult incoming phone call that he slowly stood up and then collapsed from a heart attack.

To say that conflict brings out strong human emotion is a gross understatement. Unfortunately, the only good way to manage conflict is to remove the element of emotion. Emotion is a powerful fuel in any conflict, and when it is part of the discussion mix, people can quickly start attacking each other instead of the real problem. Modest disagreement can become raging antagonism, as self-styled opponents figuratively draw lines in the sand, rage back and forth with ever greater intensity, and rarely settle anything. Obviously, managers need some sharp and effective tools to take emotion out of conflict.

Managers see it like . . .

At the first sign of manager-employee conflict, a manager might diffuse a potential difficult situation with a little tactic that we discovered during our own early experiences in management. The manager can create some distance from the conflict for everyone involved by saying, "Managers see it like," and then explaining how managers at the company would view the problematical situation. It is important to note that he did not start the conversation with "I see it like." After the management perspective has been made clear in a non-confrontational way, the manager opens the way to frank, friendly discussion by asking how employees at this company view a situation like this. Again, it is important to note that the manager did not say "How do you view the situation?" Continue the "managers see it like..." and "employees see it like..." conversation until the

conflict is resolved or at least has been turned and moved in a positive direction.

Anthropologists would refer to this type of conversation as being ethnographic, that is, seeking an open and unfiltered perspective from someone else and then learning to appreciate the differences between our own opinions and those of others. It is a human weakness to look at the world through me-centered rather than other-centered lenses. It's only human to initially assume that our way of thinking is the only way, or at least the best way, and it's only by appreciating the equally human right of others to express their own ideas and suggestions—regardless of whether we believe the other viewpoints are good or bad—that a consensus can be reached and real teamwork can be achieved.

Expressing how a category of people, i.e., managers, see a situation, then asking how another category of people, i.e., employees, see the same situation allows unique perspectives to emerge without defensiveness or anger. It is surprising, but managers and employees often adopt the tactic almost as a kind of game. Few people really want to get upset and argue. They are looking for stress-free ways to resolve conflicts and express their thoughts and feelings.

Giving tough assignments

Talk to any employee about their experiences in the workplace and you will frequently hear bitter stories of being forced to do assignments that they hated doing. But from a manager's point of view, such assignments still need to get done. On the other hand, managers sometimes are not even aware of how much an employee hates the idea of working at a particular task. Managers can solve the problem by making an easy change in the language they use to discuss the assignments.

We recommend that when the manager senses the task the person is going to be assigned is something that person would really, really, REALLY prefer not to do, the manager shifts gears from "You'll be doing..." to the less threatening, softer phrasing of "I need your help... how would you feel about..."

It's like the fireman's safety hint of feeling a door before opening it when there may be a fire raging on the other side. Placing the employee in a position of trust protects the manager from having the employee blow up. Specific examples of a soft approach to reaching out to the employee include phrases such as, "I know Christmas is next week, but I really need your help. How would you feel about going to Detroit this week and a doing some personal interviews downtown?" and "I think you are the best person for a new job opportunity. How would you feel about relocating yourself and your family to our new office in Spokane?" One of our favorites is "I am going to be out of town next week and really need someone I can trust to help out. How would you feel about teaching my Thursday classes for me."

When we start off a request with "How would you feel about...," we help ourselves by anticipating some employee pushback, but more importantly we help employees openly express concerns. Managers tell us that when employees are free to express concerns, it usually is easy to resolve those concerns. The shift in attitude from "I resent doing this" to "This is going to be tough, but my manager thinks I am a hero for doing it" makes a huge difference in employee performance, employee loyalty, and the manager's peace of mind.

Sending silly signals

People are always testing boundaries. We have developed several non-threatening ways to signal employees when they cross a boundary in the office. First, when we witness someone saying or doing something that is inappropriate under the present circumstances, we raise our eyebrows and say, "Wow! I've never heard that expressed quite like that before!" Everyone laughs and no harm is done. We raise eyebrows because people take it so personally if we lower our eyebrows . . . even if we say something mildly positive like, "That is a very interesting way to think about the problem." Go ahead and try it. When leadership eyebrows drop, people are confused. "Does the manager love me or hate me for saying that? Do we love them or hate them? We don't want people to be confused about our managerial mindset even if they do cross established and well-marked boundaries of taste, comportment or respect. We keep our eyebrows up!

When people behave in an odd or challenging way, the manager might say, "You're so funny." They usually respond, "Funny about what?" (defensive), or "Do you really think so?" (approval-seeking). The response to either of those questions might be "Yeah, I never would have thought about doing that." Usually that opens a short discussion during which manager and employee both learn to see the situation from each other's viewpoint, tension is reduced or eliminated, and that particular boundary is once again in place, and possibly more clearly marked than before.

Sometimes we may even say, "I am sorry but that is a head-slapping offense." If we can keep a smile on our face and maintain a playful tone, it often pays off to be direct about bothersome behavior. Managers write to us about lots of employee behaviors that cross reasonable boundaries. An employee who makes noises at his desk by hitting his cheeks like drums: "John, that is a head-slapping offense." An employee who chronically shows up late for meetings: "Martha, that is a head-slapping offense." A manager who goes to sleep during an employee presentation: "Gary (or Mr. Garrison," if that might be more appropriate), that is a head-slapping offense."

Not only does this sort of playful, but still meaningful type of action usually "reform" the offender, but it also reminds the rest of the office team of the existence of reasonable limits of behavior and expectations of the organization without hard words or heavy-handed memos and reminders on office bulletin boards.

Chapter SEVENTEEN

PLAY ALONG – MOVE ALONG

My idea of an agreeable person is a person who agrees with me.

Benjamin Disraeli

Ilona was among the first students to complete our leadership performance course. She is a bright, young, and attractive manager from Lithuania, and she will remain forever as one of our favorite students. She has described herself as one of those people who takes everything seriously. Before getting to know her, her classmates described her as tough and difficult. We worried about her, because she sat at the very back of the classroom with her arms folded. In Ilona's home culture, it is important to concentrate on work . . . there is no time for being social. When she first arrived in America, she remembered forcing herself to smile and listen to co-workers chitchat and tell stories as she thought to herself, "unproductive time." Lithuanians can also be very direct, especially when dealing with rude people. Ilona admitted to reacting quickly and sharply in such instances. After those occasional heated exchanges she always felt badly, she said, and looked for better ways to handle future tense situations.

She was attending our classes in the evenings, and she knew she had a tough meeting coming up with an area sales manager at her daytime job. Unsure of the skills she was learning in our leadership performance class, she asked her supervisor at the company to help her out during the meeting, but her boss just sat back as the sales manager threw out insults to attack her and her department. She explained to us later that everything happened so fast that she did not have time to come up with a defensive strategy or a clever retort.

However, she knew that for once she did not want to fight back. So she concentrated on pleasant thoughts, put a smile on her face, and just absorbed all the negativity coming at her. This was a heroic act because it was completely against her nature. Finally, as the sales manager was working up to full steam, Ilona turned directly to her attacker, nodded her head and almost apologetically said, "You are absolutely right. We do not know anything because no one has taught us, but we are willing to learn. You are much more knowledgeable than we are and with your help we should be able to overcome all of these obstacles." Her words and attitude worked a small miracle. The meeting came to an abrupt ending as the sales manager's head of steam quickly cooled down. The sales manager agreed to put together a training package, and Ilona was able to quickly get back to work and feel good about herself and the outcome. She played along so that she could move along.

Ilona learned something special that day, something we have also learned through a few difficult experiences with people who were aggressive, but not great leaders. When we (or incidentally our ideas) are being put down, sternly criticized, or even screamed at, we have a choice to either quickly move forward with positive momentum or get bogged down in a morass of bad feelings. If we put a smile on our face and play along with the negativity we can usually move on to a swift and satisfying result. If we put on a frown and fight, our positive momentum is stopped short and our cause is almost always lost. It is natural, instinctive, and protective to want to react aggressively when someone attacks the quality or quantity of our work or some other aspect of our role in the group. And we certainly don't want to just stand there with a dumfounded look, giving our antagonist the distinct feeling that we are even dumber than he had imagined.

Reacting with anger or any attempt at showing up the critic can only inject more heat into the situation, and could end any hope for continued employment. Looking stunned and helpless makes senior management wonder if the criticized fledgling manager should be trusted to do anything in the company without closer, almost invariably hostile supervision. So what must we train ourselves to do? We do not want to react defensively but we do want to act positively by playing the "play along—move along" game. This tactic can quickly defuse the situation and move the problem from a "me against you" position to a "we will have to look closer at this and see what we should both have done," face-saving solution.

The tactical delay

One manager shared a story with us about a sales meeting in which he was comparing cultivating new customers to cultivating a garden. One of the salespeople known for off-the-wall remarks spoke up and said, "You have to be very careful with gardens because in the wrong hands they can use fertilizer to make bombs." Now, in a similar situation we would have been tempted to just smile and say, "Bill, making comments like that is a head-slapping offense," and then move on. This manager, however, decided to play along by employing a tactical delay. He drew a picture of a bomb on the whiteboard and asked if it would be all right to return to the comment in a moment. As the sales meeting was coming to an end, the discussion turned to things that salespeople might do with good intentions to encourage future sales, but which often could work against future sales. At this point, the manager returned to the picture of the bomb he drew earlier and listed the comments. He summarized by highlighting all of the positive things to do to encourage sales and used the bomb picture to reinforce what can happen if salespeople push some otherwise good things too far.

The tactical delay can be very effective because we don't always immediately know how to correctly leverage the outrageous comments that people make. However, we can't recall even one instance in which we were not able to make something positive out of some *non sequitur* or otherwise outrageous remark. Once we put up the remark for everyone to see, it just stares at us, challenging our creativity to find a way to use it!

Let everyone play along

Peer pressure is a wonderful thing. Leaders may look like they are standing up by themselves, but they never are, and the great leaders are quick to admit it. We have a lot of people out there to help us. A manager of a customer service center led a short team meeting every morning before starting the day. One morning he was giving the announcements to the team when one of the service representatives started finishing all of his sentences. The employee was definitely a member of the Hate Group who had been hired only because of pressure applied by his father, who held an influential position in the company. Even though this employee was a low performer, he was very knowledgeable. He corrected others constantly, but didn't take correction very well himself, a fairly common condition among people like this. When the employee started acting out, the manager acted even more quickly and invited the whole team to play along. He asked everyone to start completing his sentences. He brilliantly used the collective power of the group and turned a tense situation into something fun and memorable.

Chapter EIGHTEEN

EXPLORE

The greatest obstacle to discovery is not ignorance—it is the illusion of knowledge.

Daniel J. Boorstin

T he root cause of our anxiety when stepping out in front of an audience is most likely our fear of criticism. Most people are very uncomfortable when others criticize them in public. But criticism, when it is constructive, and it is applied to getting the work done, and not to humiliate an individual or build the critic's self-esteem, is important. Speaking for most real management professionals, we love criticism. We want criticism. We invite criticism. We encourage people to openly attack our ideas. Truthfully, we have had to get used to it. But we do know that negative energy in an

"Memo to self: Tell company cafeteria to take tomatoes off the menu."

XEBEC INDUSTRIES ANNUAL EMPLOYEE MEETING

© BYU Academic Publishing

organization is better than no energy at all.

It is easy to come up with examples of students being intimidated by professors who wear virtual blinders to criticism. One professor who we know occasionally can make students feel quite uneasy. One day in class he said, "Having problems with a professor for the way he teaches a class is a lot like serving a roasted dog for Thanksgiving dinner to your relatives. Everyone sees it on the table and knows what it is, but no one wants to say anything about it." He then left the room and instructed the students to talk about any issues that they might have with him or the course.

When he returned the students didn't have much to say. They were still afraid of how he might react. One student, however, mustered the courage to say that the whole exercise was nothing but a waste of time. Hearing the comment, the professor got angry and dismissed the class for the day. We think that anecdote is a true classic. The professor conducted an exercise to demonstrate that he was open to criticism, and then when one student took him at his word and he was criticized he got angry and dismissed the class.

Every leader faces objections and rejection. Like it or not, we are carefully measured—and remembered—by how we act or react. To survive leadership, we must learn how to turn negative energy into positive energy. Consider the example of a young lady sitting in the back of a conference room. Most of the time she is either not paying attention or has her arms folded. Finally, her objections to the presentation come to a head and she raises her hand and remarks, "All of the things you are talking about are so naïve. We would have to do a much more careful analysis to be able to solve the problems you're talking about."

The speaker plays along with her comments as the negative energy builds. He then says, "Margaret, you may be right. Perhaps what we are doing is too simple to get us where we need to be." He turns to a young man sitting in the middle row. "Richard, what do you think? Can you provide some support for Margaret?" Richard replies, "Well, I do think we are leaving out some important points." The speaker next says, "Gee, I guess we could be missing some important things about the problem." He then continues, "Well great. Let's make a list of what we're leaving out." He then involves the whole group in listing some additional points that the attendees feel should be considered. Next he calls everyone's attention to the agenda and says, "Margaret and Richard are right. We do need to push our thinking quite a bit further. I'm probably moving through the material too slowly. I didn't realize how quickly everyone is catching on. Let's move right on to address all of these additional points. But before we go forward, I really want to thank Margaret for leading us into this discussion. I think it's been very valuable!"

From that point forward, Margaret became one of the speaker's biggest fans. She sat on the edge of her seat ready to contribute. She immediately came to his defense when others turned critical. Margaret had come to the conference with a lot of energy and that gave her the potential to become a great advocate. The speaker only needed to recognize her potential, play along with her initial negativity, show confidence in her thinking skills, and finally turn her early negative energy into positive energy.

There is "right" in every "wrong" remark

Negative energy that gets people excited and thinking "outside the box" is a priceless commodity in any organization. Employee objections give a Plus-One leader some of the best opportunities to forcefully put across what should be said in a training or team-building meeting. A project manager ran into her supervisor's office, agitated and demanding to be heard. She said that all the company management sucks and the company has no chance for surviving. Her manager calmly replied, "I can think of many reasons why management sucks, but please be more specific about how you think management sucks." She shot back that one of the new salespeople had offered a customer a statement of work that included a $200,000 guarantee that a new product would be in production in less than two months. She continued that the guarantee was impossible because the new product's production depended on many third-party vendors that could not be controlled.

Once the supervisor knew her real concern, it was easy to manage. He contacted the sales group and said if they could guarantee the $200,000 from their own sales budget they would do their very best to meet the short deadline. The outcome was good all around—the project manager calmed down, the sales team retracted the guarantee, and the new salesperson who made the unrealistic guarantee learned a valuable lesson.

Shockingly simple solutions

When managers have the courage to explore negativity, they often are amazed at how tense situations can be quickly turned around with shockingly simple solutions. One manager reports that his executive team conducts a company-wide poll of employee attitudes every 12 to 18 months. For the first time in memory, his area of the business recently scored substantially lower than the over-all company average. He thought he'd been OB'd!

The manager's first inclination was to ignore the results and move on with business as usual. He feared that open discussions with employees would be a lightning rod for every little frustration and pet peeve. He admitted that ultimately the employees staged a mini-rebellion because they wanted to know why management was not discussing the survey results and soliciting suggestions. The employees sent a "personal message" with the survey and wanted to make sure that management got it.

Eventually, he reluctantly conducted meetings that explored their concerns. Fortunately, the manager had spent years building good rapport with the employees. Although it was painful, he kept smiling and listened carefully to all the sessions' gripes. After two meetings, the growing rift between sales and the support staff emerged as the most troubling issue. The discussions had originally centered on differences in pay and incentives between sales and support staff, but it soon became apparent that the support staff was hurt the most by the salespeople not acknowledging their efforts to help create customer satisfaction and loyalty. The consensus of the group was that a good first step would be if each salesperson would quit referring to a customer as "my account" and in the future refer to them as "our account." Of course, that minor change in language was only a first step, but the manager was struck with how simple it was to start building positive momentum in the organization. He wondered why he had put off talking with employees about the survey results. The results were much more positive than he anticipated. He was beginning to believe in the Explore tactic.

Golden opportunities

Negative comments like "I don't agree with what you are saying" or "That's not true" are often great opportunities to energize the work group. As you hone your skills and develop your Plus-One abilities, look for those opportunities, cherish them and nourish them. And after gaining confidence, you might even try to cause them occasionally just to see what happens. Using mental "kung fu" to throw the negative energy of the sender back like a boomerang to stimulate the whole group can be one of your most powerful management tools! Start exploring to build positive group momentum by using the following steps:

1. Never take negative comments personally or directly. Think of innocent criticism and mean-spirited personal attacks both as the opening round of a moderately risky, but extremely enjoyable game where you can frequently learn something valuable.

2. Play along with the negative energy and then encourage a thoughtful discussion on the topic with input from everyone and then listen for positive energy.

3. Always involve the whole group to find out where they stand on the issue. "Do you think John is right?" "Where do the rest of you stand on this issue?"

4. Once you identify the positive energy, turn the initial criticisms around to become a positive force for change and consensus building.

5. Reinforce the contribution of the critics to the discussion. Assure these individuals that they are appreciated and that their comments are helping the group to move in the right direction.

Part FOUR

Engaging the Fence Sitters

Part FOUR

Engaging the Fence Sitters

A group of MBA students were taking a class on creativity at an Ivy League school. Of course, every person in the room felt gifted and creative, so when the professor gave them a problem to solve everyone was eager to show off what they could do. "There is a ping-pong ball sitting at the bottom of a steel pipe," the professor explained. "The pipe is about a foot long and is set upright in a concrete floor. The pipe has a wide-enough diameter to let the ping-pong ball easily slide down to the bottom of the pipe. You are to remove the ping-pong ball from the pipe, and to do this, you are given a box of tools to accomplish the task. Your tools include a pair of long-necked scissors, a ball of string, a Band-Aid, chewing gum, and a plastic straw. The room is otherwise empty, but you are allowed to use anything in the room, inside or outside of your toolbox, to retrieve the ping-pong ball from the bottom of that pesky pipe."

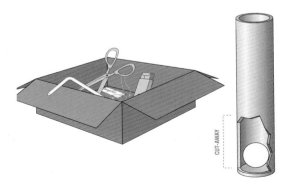

CUT-AWAY

- Scissors
- String
- Band-aid
- Chewing Gum
- Soda Straw

"Now," smiled the professor, "divide up quickly into teams, each with four students. Your team will compete with the other teams to determine how to remove the ping-pong ball from the pipe." The professor then quickly added, "When each team has decided on a solution, we will match your solutions with answers given by engineers interviewing for a job at a leading technology firm!"

The students immediately formed little groups and started to brainstorm. In a few minutes the professor called for everyone's attention and called for solutions. Hands went up and student puzzlemeisters eagerly offered their solutions.

"Suck the ball out with the straw," one person suggested. "Fish the ball out with gum on the end of the string," another offered. Answers really started flying. Students suggested that the ball be skewered with the scissors, that someone just blow down the pipe, or blow across the top of the pipe, or put the Band-Aid on the end of the straw and snag the ball, and one particularly brawny student even offered to simply break off the pipe.

At this point the professor held up his hand and stopped the discussion. He smiled and asked everyone if they were ready to compare their answers with those given by the engineers. "Yeah," a few people bellowed, while the rest just nodded their approval. "Well," the professor beamed, "you covered all the answers—you even thought of the ones mentioned by just a few of the engineers taking this little test." He waited while the class applauded their own cleverness and traded high fives. Then he leaned well over his lectern and said in a low voice, "Unfortunately, none of your imaginative and

TOP ANSWERS

85%	PUT THE GUM ON THE END OF STRING AND "FISH OUT" BALL	60%	SUCK OUT THE BALL WITH THE STRAW
70%	BLOW DOWN THE PIPE UNTIL THE BALL POPS OUT	57%	BLOW OVER THE PIPE UNTIL THE BALL COMES OUT
65%	PUT THE BAND-AID ON THE END OF THE STRAW	45%	TAKE THE SCISSORS APART, TIE ONE-HALF TO THE STRING, AND SKEWER THE BALL

numerous answers offered today would have removed the ball from the pipe. None of these answers actually work under real-life conditions." After a pause to let that sink in, the professor continued. "However, I know there must be at least one student sitting in this classroom today who knows the right solution!"

The professor continued, "You're probably just a little embarrassed to say it, but it's okay; you can say anything in this class as long as it's on topic." A young man sitting on the front row then raised his hand and explained, "I think the tools are just to divert everyone from thinking really creatively. To remove the ping-pong ball from the pipe without using anything from outside the room, everyone on the team could just pee in the pipe and the ball would float to the top." The professor smiled broadly. "That's right. Just add water from—ahem— any available source!" As the slightly deflated students sank back in their seats and figuratively pounded themselves on their heads, the professor summed up the purpose of the exercise by pointing out, "Creative answers usually come out when we force ourselves to think outside the box we are given, and we start looking around to find new tools or new methods that may be better-suited to the particular task at hand."

That professor's little exercise is a good example of a tactic we call "lean and smack." We'll describe it in more detail later in this section of the book. This tactic's main purpose is to engage the Swing Group that exists in every organization, regardless of size and type.

Fence sitting is a popular sport

The Swing Group sits on the fence. They like the view from up there. At the top of the fence they can think about everything in the world, except, of course, what you are trying to explain, achieve or plan for. Members of the Swing Group are preoccupied, indifferent and often unresponsive—and the really bad news is that they usually make up more than half of your employees. The Swing Group is very effective at filtering out messages, as are most people in modern society. We've read that about 1600 different ads are shown on television in America each day. Of these 1600 ads, it is estimated that about 25 are remembered and of those 25 only 16 make a positive impression. Our society is awash in a wave of messages and diversions. To stay afloat each of us early on develops a communications callus to protect us from the complexity and distractions we face each day. This callus is thick and difficult to cut through, which is bad news for managers and leaders. If we can't grab the attention of the individuals with whom we must work, we simply can't get things done the way they should and could be done.

Information overload forces people to make choices about what they listen to. We all know that there is too much going on for us to take it all in. But when we are trying to motivate and lead others, we need to be aware ahead of time of several common situations in which people are almost guaranteed not to pay attention.

Criticism doesn't get the right kind of attention

We want to avoid those times when we feel the need to get up in front of people and tell them that they are doing poorly. It's only natural to want to do this, and it's also only natural, when people are told they are doing poorly, for them to say to themselves, "I'm doing poorly, the boss says. I'm going to continue to do poorly. Why waste my time trying to change? It's boring. That task is not worth doing anyway."

The exception is the person who actually wants to focus on improving when they are told they are doing something poorly. These rare people in the workforce will find a way to improve their performance, and thus succeed, no matter who is doing the leading. Yet we know that we often act as if the exception is the rule. A more typical story is that of a young woman who dropped out of freshman English twice because she "couldn't get it," but then made a B in the class when she took it from an instructor named Bill Shakespeare. This professor enthusiastically supported everything she did and perhaps because of his name, she found his class more interesting and engaging than she would have otherwise.

Today's managers and leaders are competing for employee "air-time," or as we prefer to call it, "mindshare." That somewhat omi-nous-sounding compound word is not the same as "brainwashing," and despite the obvious definition, it has nothing to do with the man-ager somehow getting control of either side of your brain. In "mind-share," we simply want to make sure everyone involved in the task or project is not only "on the same page," but is actively following our finger down the page. We have identified five surefire tactics to win the battle for mindshare. When you stand up in front of your employ-ees, you are supposed to already know everything you need to know about your product, topic, or task. Your employees assume this so you'd better not disappoint them. Beyond that, the tactics we will describe here simply help to make what you have to say more vivid, engaging and memorable. But before we get to these tactics, let's spend some time learning a few things about demotivation and the American worker.

Chapter NINETEEN

DEMOTIVATORS AND THE AMERICAN WORKER

A person may cause evil to others not only by his actions but by his inaction, and in either case he is justly accountable to them for the injury.

John Stuart Mill

Before you, as a manager, can start motivating your team or your workers, you must first learn to stop demotivating them. In his book on motivation, Dean Spitzer lists twenty-one things that managers do that demotivate workers.[1] We were fascinated by the list, so we asked a group of 50 managers to rate each of the twenty-one demotivators on two dimensions—first, how personally painfully or troublesome they felt the demotivator had been in their experience, and second, how easy they think the demotivator would be to fix.

The manager's best chance for engaging the Swing Group is to carefully avoid the "high pain" demotivators, particularly those that are perceived to be easily fixed. Of course, one can imagine that even popular managers who too frequently offend workers with this deadly list of don'ts could alienate their organization's Love Group.

---

1.   *Super-Motivation* by Dean Spitzer

	EASY TO FIX	DIFFICULT TO FIX
HIGH PAIN	Discouraging Comments Unnecessary Rules Unclear Expectations Taken for Granted Criticism	Manager Hypocrisy Over-Control Manager Dishonesty Unfairness Office Politics Taking Away Benefits
MODERATE PAIN	Forced to Do Poor Quality Poorly Designed Work Withholding Information Unproductive Meetings Lack of Follow-up Management Invisibility	Underutilizing Skills Unhealthy Competition Tolerating Poor Quality Constant Change

With so many demotivators already affecting their lives, people often have a hard time sensing movement or progress, day-to-day. Salespeople have this problem when the sales cycle is long. Employees have this problem when they don't have a good way to keep score of their little daily achievements. In general, people cannot make a connection between what they can do now, what they have done in the past, and what they will be able to do in the future. It is really a problem of continuity. When people do not feel a sense of positive continuity, when they cannot get a sense of where their efforts are taking them, they stop listening and they stop trying. Without some means of measurement we seldom gain the motivation we need to improve our day-to-day performance. Plus-One leaders make special efforts to help people know how far they have progressed.

We've often seen really outstanding leaders address this pesky measurement or continuity problem by asking their employees three simple "linking" questions:

1. Where are we?

2. Where have we come from?

3. Where are we going?

Sound familiar? These questions are important in every aspect of life, and to every individual, as well as to every group and organization with a common cause or mission to perform. As leaders we therefore need to make it easy for people to track their progress. We need to provide "roadmaps," "scorecards," "milestones," "landmarks" and everything else we might be able to think up which might make it easy for people to recognize the good things they are doing with their specific assignments, their careers and their lives. **The key is to avoid demotivators while providing positive feedback that people are improving**.

The forms of feedback we are accustomed to in our society are almost exclusively negative. It starts when we are five or six and go to school for the first time and it continues on and on throughout our lives. Teachers use grades to provide feedback, but grades provide primarily negative feedback. Even people that get 95 percent of the material correct will dwell on the five percent they got wrong rather than on the 95 percent that they got right. People are funny like that! All of us whose managerial job description includes providing feedback can learn a lesson from test grades and their built-in negativity. Negative feedback, despite its intended results, simply does not give a six-year-old, or a college student, or an individual halfway through a career a sense of forward movement or progress. It stops most people dead in their tracks.

We frequently work with customer service centers, and we find that the feedback systems in place there are almost exclusively negative. Employees already know where they stand, but what they really need to know is how far they have come. The scorecards set up by managers in these centers always measure "how many," rarely "how well," and never "how far." This can be a real problem, because we've found that the negative feedback has a negative effect on employee morale (explaining the high employee turn-over rate in many of these centers) and the overall quality of service provided by the organization.

When we look at this issue in a company, we divide employees into four categories. First, there are the "tigers," those who excel at "how many" and "how well." Second, there are the "kittens," those who lag far behind on "how many" and "how well." Third, there are the "foxes," those who shine on "how many," but do poorly on "how well." Fourth, there are the "puppies," those who shine on "how well," but do poorly on "how many."

Organizations that exclusively rely on negative feedback primarily retain only two types of employees, foxes and kittens. Foxes stay because they learn how to beat the system. In customer service jobs, they win the "how many" game by quickly hanging up on incoming calls from customers that sound as if they may be angry (fast, impatient breathing). Foxes try to handle only the easiest problems themselves, and find ways to quickly pass off difficult problems to other service representatives who are "better at handling that kind of problem."

On the other hand, kittens stay because the negative feedback starts them believing they are not very good at anything they do and so they feel they are lucky to have a job at all. Kittens listen carefully to criticism. They feel they deserve it. As we've said, they are just happy to have a job and accept as a type of religious penance the humiliation that comes from their negative feedback. The other two types of employees, tigers and puppies, often move on as soon as they can to work in environments in which the feedback systems are more positive. We want to give the people we manage and work with a sense of what they are doing well. We also want to show them that they are learning and making progress. We want everyone to understand that we all make mistakes, and that we all are operating at dif-

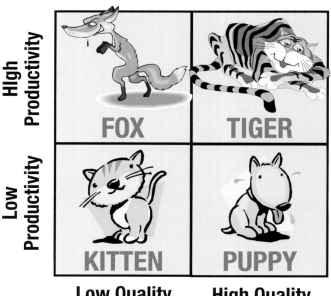

ferent levels of efficiency and competency, but also that we all are moving forward.

One solution to the difficult problem of providing positive feedback in a negative feedback society centers around the use of those three linking questions: Where are we? Where have we come from? Where are we going? Motivational feedback is dynamic. It has movement. For example, several months ago one of us signed up with a physical fitness center. The first thing the center did was to test our arm, leg and abdominal strength. Then they told us that based on our weight, age, and gender, we fell into the 30th percentile. That's O.K., we thought. We've never been to a gym before and we aren't particularly athletic. After three months of following the gym instructor's suggested regimen of physical workouts we were measured again. Now we were in the 60th percentile. We knew we were getting stronger because each week we were able to handle a little more weight, but it was great to be able to quantify the improvement. It gave us a sense of how far we had come and how much we could continue to improve over the next three-month period. With this feedback system we did not dwell on what we couldn't do. Our thoughts were automatically focused on making progress. Our goal was to focus on the 95 percent that we were doing right rather than on the five percent that we didn't yet have quite right!

It is easy for employees to lose their way. It is also easy for employees not to recognize the progress they have already made. An effective manager needs to point out how high they have climbed on the mountain. From time to time we should stop and rest to review progress and look ahead to see how high we can climb if we keep following the path. Asking linking questions, or better yet, developing a positive feedback system that incorporates the linking questions gives leaders the tools to demonstrate that their people are getting better and more capable day by day.

Chapter TWENTY

SURPRISE PILES

---

*Laughter is the closest distance
between two people.*

Victor Borge

Every now and then a really good leader needs to shake people up with a surprise or two. "Surprise piles" is the name for the little things we can do to shock people out of their comfortable rhythm. This tactic is like a "mental alarm clock" or like a cold bucket of water splashed in the face. Surprise piles keep people listening, learning and doing even during the occasional dry period. The tactic is frequently used to (1) shock people out of a trance and get them back into the game, (2) focus attention on key points that are critical to the task, and (3) make the key points memorable for weeks, months, or even years after they have been said.

When one of our colleagues introduces seminar attendees to the special problems associated with international business she likes to wake up her listeners with a few advertising slogans or product names from other countries. One of her favorites is the advertising used to market Electrolux vacuum cleaners in the U.K. The slogan is "Nothing sucks like an Electrolux." As you might imagine, that shakes up everyone who has grown up here in the U.S. The group wonders why

Electrolux would use such an outrageous slogan in Britain. They say, "The British speak English. Wouldn't the slogan sound just as bad to them as it does to us?" Other favorites are the Chevy Nova. When it was marketed in Mexico, none of the English-speaking-only marketing people realized that "Nova," translated into Spanish, means "no go."

She might also rhetorically ask her seminar audience to just imagine how much business Brooklyn's Jun Kee Auto Repair Shop might be getting. And for possible reasons why Japan's second largest travel agency, Kinki Nippon Tourist Company, decided to change its name after doing business in the U.S. for less than a year. These "surprise piles" are humorous, but they also make an important point about the impact of culture and brand name on the success of a product, and the importance of really knowing who you're talking to.

Spice it up with humor

When we talk about customer service, we should mention that we've also found some ways to wake people up in that area of the business world. Everyone knows it is important to satisfy the customer. We bring the concept to life when we show a letter that Clyde Barrow, of the famous 1930s' bank-robbing duo, Bonnie and Clyde, may have written to Henry Ford. Clyde is said to have sent a personal letter to thank Ford for building such a fast and reliable automobile.

In Clyde's line of work, speed and vehicle reliability were of course critical. We also point out that it is the little things in customer service that can often make a big difference in customer satisfaction. Quality is all about doing a hundred small things right, and when we stress that point, everyone's response is just about always, "yeah, yeah, yeah. We've heard all of this before." Except we know that people don't really understand the concept even if they have heard it before.

To drive the point home, we give them a real life "surprise pile" using a credit card application. "Poor Professor Whitlark," we say. "He just doesn't get much respect. Let's take a look at a credit card application he got in the mail. Here's one from Visa. Now," we tell our listeners, "Everyone repeat the name on the card application." The

"I started out with the Love Group, but it was the Hate Group that inspired me to blow up the Suggestion Box."

© BYU Academic Publishing

audience slowly sounds out the name exactly as it appears on the card, "D. Whitlard." We then ask, "Would you apply and use this card?" The listeners reply, "Absolutely not. They didn't spell his name right and it sounds like they are making fun of him." "Precisely," we say, "who would want to be called by that name?" Even the smallest mistakes in quality can have a major impact on customer satisfaction and on a company's ability to get consumers to take action."

Take a risk and do something memorable

It is difficult for a leader to be memorable if that leader's behavior is always traditional and unremarkable. When he was 42, Soichiro Honda started manufacturing motorcycles as the president of the now famous Honda Corporation. Many people believe that his personal drive, genius and unique style of leadership turned Honda into the best-selling motorcycle manufacturer in the world. So the story goes, Mr. Honda once stripped naked and assembled a motorcycle on top of a work bench in front of a group of company engineers just to make a point that they would never forget! This was outrageous behavior for anyone, but particularly in the Japanese culture, where

© Honda Corporation

Be Memorable

Soichiro Honda, the founder of the Honda Corporation, was one of the nicest people his engineers ever met!

it is commonly said that "the nail that sticks out is hammered down." Yet, there is little doubt that the engineers listened to and understood Mr. Honda's message and of course the success of the company speaks for itself.

Surprise Piles don't need to be sophisticated to be effective. Spicing up a dry presentation with an appropriately-themed cartoon, wearing a t-shirt to a team meeting with a humorous message tied to team goals, or even dressing up like Santa and giving out recognition awards all can help what you say cut through and be memorable.

It is hard to carry the idea of a Surprise Pile too far. For years one business professor at the Darden Business School started off a case study about chainsaws by cutting a chair in two. Understandably, people were on the edge of their seats throughout the entire activity!

Chapter TWENTY-ONE

STUMP THE MANAGER

The only factor becoming scarce in a world of abundance is human attention.

Kevin Kelly

Have you ever wondered why so many employees never seem to do things "by the book?" Why do customer service centers need to pay "quality control supervisors" to monitor phone calls just to make sure the service representatives are following the approved procedures? There are probably a lot of explanations, but the one that answers this question best is also the simplest:

Who Wants to Be a Millionaire? © ABC Television

Learning is painful. For employees to do things "by the book," they first need to learn everything in the book and that's painful. It has been said that education is the one product for which people will pay more to get less.

Using the Surprise Pile tactic will help people remember the highlights, but now that is not enough. We are in need of more powerful medicine to get people to learn the vast amounts of

"The idea is to dunk the boss, not hold him under!"

detail required to successfully run a modern business. When faced with this situation, we break our own rules and purposely put ourselves up on a pedestal and encourage, even reward, people to knock us off. We play Stump the Manager. It is like a quiz game where the prize is "showing up" your boss. Businesses can't afford to give their employee "contestants" huge sums of money, like the quiz show "Who Wants to Be a Millionaire," but the prospect of knocking a manager off their perch is very tempting if not downright delicious!

Quiz shows were born on radio 70 years ago and have been a worldwide staple of family entertainment ever since. Quiz show experts believe that the format appeals to people because everyone can compete vicariously and when they know the answer, they enjoy congratulating themselves. Whatever the reason, Stump the Manager is engaging. It's like combining the elements of a quiz show with another American favorite, the Celebrity Dunking Booth. It's difficult to get managers to experiment with Stump the Manager. It must be a problem with human evolution that causes us to climb up on a pedestal when we shouldn't and shy away from climbing up on a pedestal when we should. It may be a little frightening, from a manager's perspective, to encourage employees to hurl hardballs which, sooner or later, are sure to connect. But this is one time getting knocked down helps the manager—and therefore the entire organization—much more than it hurts the manager. You can prepare yourself by being in the right mindset when you finally decide to play Stump the Manager. That way you won't react defensively when challenged and when finally defeated. If you're in the right mindset you will laugh, say something like, "You stumped me with that one," and reward the challenger for their flawless aim and bullseye hit. From that point on, you will find many employees will want to be *the* expert that can stump you. You will also discover them saying some positive things like, "Our boss is not so stuffy after all." The employee attitude will have been born out of good sportsmanship, not out of resentment. With our love of quiz shows, knocking people off from their high horse, and competition, any other attitude would be almost un-American!

Here is an example of how we have used the Stump the Manager tactic to teach business teams how to do some marketing research. Getting managers to better understand customer value is one of our favorite training topics. The goal of the exercise in this case is to understand one's best customers well enough to successfully make substantive improvements to the business' current set of products and services. To accomplish the task the business team must conduct a rather complex set of personal interviews[2] with several of their best customers. When making the assignment, we provide a general set of questions that must be answered by the personal interviews rather than provide the less time-consuming handout, a step-by-step cookbook. For example, we ask the business team to identify the benefits different customers want most when they are buying products in a particular category, the attributes of the product that most effectively deliver those benefits, the personal reasons for benefits being important to the customer, and the personal values activated by those personal reasons.

2.   *Understanding Consumer Decision-Making: A Means-End Approach to Marketing and Advertising Strategy* edited by Reynolds and Olson

As one might imagine, getting that kind of information from people is not easy. But without further instruction, we ask the business team to conduct some practice interviews. We also give them a couple of journal articles for reference. After completing their practice interviews, the business team reconvenes and we ask everyone how they did. In general, the team members say they still don't get it. So we send them away to read the reference articles which, by the way, provide excellent step-by-step problem-solving tips for the exercise. We say that when they return, the two of us will be the experts on the research method and that the team can try to stump us. If someone stumps us, and someone invariably will, we just smile and hand out a reward. Then we ask for the team to find or suggest an answer based on the reference material. After the exercise, the business team is well equipped to do the research. They feel confident. They know where to go to find answers to questions that might come up. And perhaps best of all, we never had to lecture, and they never had to feel bored, indifferent, or drop off to sleep.

Chapter TWENTY-TWO

THOUGHTS AND FEELINGS

The illiterate of the 21st century will not be those who cannot read and write, but those that cannot learn, unlearn and relearn.

Alvin Toffler

Just when are those times that an astute manager really wants people in his or her organization to listen, remember and act? New employee training? Announced changes in policy and/or clarification of policy? When outlining project goals and responsibilities? When motivating employees to perform better? When was the last time someone tried to get you to listen, remember, and act in your job? How did they do it? How soon was your mind wandering? How did they go about numbing your mind and putting you to sleep? Chances are they lectured because lecturing is the easiest thing to do. On the other hand, maybe you nodded in and out of consciousness while you were reading a company manual. Perhaps the lights were dimmed and you slept right through a PowerPoint presentation or training video.

Consider this all-to-common story of an employee at a local store. The owner of the business is quite analytical, i.e., Robotic, so when his frustration with employees builds to the point for the need to change or clarify work policy rather than speaking to the problem directly, he types up a few pages of instructions which he hands out to each employee to read and "sign off" on, to acknowledge that they understand it. Everyone reads it, of course, and everyone signs it, of course. And of course, it's no surprise to find out that no one remembers it. So a copy of the policy is kept in the "emergency box" just in case the owner quizzes them about the "new" way of doing things.

Fact is, as your chance of sleeping or otherwise being distracted increases, your chance of remembering anything helpful decreases. The well-known Learning Pyramid is a stark reminder of how ineffective we can be as leaders unless we adopt new and perhaps uncomfortable ways to communicate.

As communicators, our goal should be to attain at least 50% retention of delivered information. So we know from the outset that lecturing, reading assignments and PowerPoint presentations in and of themselves—or even used in combination—will not get us anywhere near our 50% goal. We are always looking for tools that will help us engage people in active, and therefore stimulating, memorable discussion.

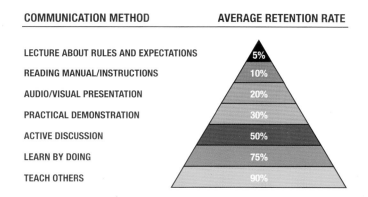

COMMUNICATION METHOD	AVERAGE RETENTION RATE
LECTURE ABOUT RULES AND EXPECTATIONS	5%
READING MANUAL/INSTRUCTIONS	10%
AUDIO/VISUAL PRESENTATION	20%
PRACTICAL DEMONSTRATION	30%
ACTIVE DISCUSSION	50%
LEARN BY DOING	75%
TEACH OTHERS	90%

Transform presentations into focus groups

When we have worked with political candidates we often video tape a speech and then replay it for a "focus group," which is com-

posed of an audience of likely voters. Each voter receives a small box with a dial on it. They turn the dial to the right every time they have positive thoughts and feelings about the presentation to which they are being exposed. They turn the dial to the left every time they have negative feelings. The stronger the feelings the farther they turn the dial. Afterwards, we replay the videotaped speech together with a superimposed line moving up (positive) and down (negative) on the television screen to reflect the attitudes of the people in the focus group. If the line quickly rises, we pause the playback to ask about the positive thoughts and feelings that created the positive reaction. Of course, when the line quickly falls we again pause the tape and probe the negative reactions. Inviting people to watch, listen and discuss their thoughts and feelings accomplishes several things. First, people pay attention because they know the group will be asked to discuss their reactions and they want to be able to participate. Secondly, the speaker gets invaluable feedback. We've seen the course of political campaigns turn from negative to positive based on the results of this "thoughts and feelings" exercise.

Of course, in a corporate organizational setting we can't give our employees dials to turn left and right to "vote" on our comments every time we have something to say. On the other hand, when we hit one of those situations in which it is vital for us to get across a message, we can accomplish nearly the same thing by having employees take notes about positive and negative thoughts and feelings they have about what we are saying. Afterwards, we probe and discuss the notes they have made. When we do this exercise for an organization, we make sure we hear both positive and negative thoughts and feelings. Ideally everyone makes a contribution. However, at a minimum, we make sure that as many people as possible take part in the discussion.

Get Out the Garbage—Part deux

Eliciting "thoughts and feelings" from members in this kind of group and then discussing what the people in the group say is another way to "get out the garbage." But in this case, we are creating the garbage as we speak. It is humbling to realize that most everything a leader says or does bumps up against negative baggage, personal limitations and glaring omissions. The same rules apply for this second version of "get out the garbage," but now you have more skills to draw upon. Acknowledge positive comments with gratitude and humility. Of course, we call that "being like Columbo," the seemingly incompetent and bumbling TV police detective who somehow always catches the clever crook. Then address negative comments by just playing along and exploring when necessary. (A wrinkled trench coat isn't necessary.) Make notes but don't climb on a pedestal, and don't be defensive. Most important, have fun and make sure your employees know you're enjoying the give and take. If you have fun, the employees will also have fun and think more of you for the experience.

In an executive training program, we ask business teams to work together for two days, learning and talking about improving their competitive position in the marketplace. They carefully discuss their competitors, their customers and their own business. They talk about problems and solutions. The highlight of the program is when we have the team leader stand up and outline a plan of action. All the team members have pads of paper. They listen to the plan, take notes of the parts most important to them and then discuss their "thoughts and feelings." We have found that even after two days of discussions at this level, it is not unusual after one of these "thoughts and feelings" sessions for the team leader to discover that their understanding of what needs to be done to improve the business is quite different from the understanding of their business team. As managers, we all seem to operate in carefully chosen business suits, nice ties, and enormous blinders.

Chapter TWENTY-THREE

TEAM DEBATE

*Honest disagreement is often
a good sign of progress.*

Gandhi

S ometimes employees are so numb and/or reluctant to discuss sensitive issues in a group setting that nothing will do but to stage a debate. Everyone likes a good fight. It attracts attention. It gets everyone involved. When McCann-Erickson dreamed up Miller Lite's "Tastes great, less filling" advertising campaign they had a winner. How do we know that? If you watched nationally televised sports in the 1980s the short commercials of football heroes debating back and forth about whether the same brew "tastes great" or is "less filling" is hard to forget, whether you drink or not, and even though the ads haven't been shown on TV in over 20 years. In just five years of running those ads, Miller Lite sales increased over four-fold. It was the most extraordinary growth in sales ever chalked up by a beer company. The campaign remains #8 on Advertising Age's 100 Best Ad Campaigns of the 20th Century and #4 on the Top 10 list of ad slogans. So debate works. Why not bring that sort of energy to your business?

"Do I hear the welcome sound of progress out here?"

© BYU Academic Publishing

Getting everyone involved

Good managers want to get everyone involved in debating an issue. Watching two people go at each other is not enough. To get active participation from all employees, special rules for the debate have to be put in to place. Mel Silberman[3] has suggested a debate format that we think is so good we have adapted it for your study and use in your own managerial careers:

1. Write a statement defining a position regarding a sensitive issue related to your business. For example, "To encourage fast sales growth, Sporty Motorworks should immediately drop its sticker price on custom-made roadsters by 30%."

2. Divide the business team into two debating teams. Randomly assign the "pro" and "con" positions with a coin toss.

3. Depending on the size of the business team, create two or three subgroups within each debate team. Assign each subgroup to develop a list of arguments in favor of its position. Ask each subgroup to appoint a spokesperson.

---

3.   *Active Learning: 101 Strategies to Teach any Subject* by Mel Silberman

4. Set up chairs for each spokesperson so that opposing debate teams face each other. Place the remaining employees behind their respective spokespeople.

5. Begin the debate by having each spokesperson present an opening argument. Let the "con" spokesperson talk first. Ask each spokesperson to make additional remarks rather than merely reiterating what has already been said.

6. After everyone has presented their opening arguments, stop the debate and ask the subgroups to reconvene. Ask the subgroups to discuss how to counter the opening arguments of the opposition. Have each subgroup pick a new spokesperson.

7. Resume the debate. Let the "pro" spokesperson talk first. Make sure each side takes turns. Encourage the other employees to pass notes forward to help their spokespeople with arguments and/or rebuttals. Encourage the other employees to cheer when their spokespeople make particularly good arguments or rebuttals.

8. When it appears that all the key issues and possible solutions have been discussed, end the debate. Do not declare a winner, but reconvene the business team, and if possible, have everyone pull their chairs into a big circle. Start a discussion about what the employees felt were the best arguments raised, what they learned from the exercise, and how best to outline an appropriate path to make decisions to efficiently and effectively resolve the roadster pricing issue (assuming that is a real issue in your business).

The debate plan, when it's organized as above and deals with real organizational concerns, works well to bring out ideas and perspectives that may not otherwise be considered (remember our managerial blinders thought). It also stimulates all participants' thinking along the lines that are most important to organizational long-term success. We really like using a team debate to address sensitive issues and encourage all leaders to do the same. The last thing a good leader wants to do when dealing with a controversial issue is to personally take a stand, draw a line in the sand and force his or her position on the business team. That management style may be interpreted by those who do it as strong leadership, but years of watching "strong" leaders self-destruct and after having a few melt-downs ourselves, we are convinced that way is just a recipe for disaster. Why? Even if the leader is right, such coercive action will empower the Hate Group to rally support among the Swing Group. It's only wisdom without ego to use the team debate to provide some distance between yourself and the issue. Let the business team debate the issue. Let the business teams fight out the details. Managers can step back and equitably referee the process. As leaders, we personally have always felt better off when assuming the role of Solomon rather than Saddam.

Teach good sportsmanship

Sometimes, in the heat of debate competition, employees can lose their perspective and forget that they are just debating. To help everyone learn and practice good sportsmanship we hand out a set of "top ten" debating rules. You may want to develop your own top ten list designed around the personalities of your business team. This is ours:

1. Avoid the words NEVER and ALWAYS.

2. Resist the urge to say YOU'RE WRONG.

3. Concede trivial points and don't disagree with obvious truths.

4. Argue against an idea, but don't attack the person offering the idea.

5. Use SOME and not MANY or MOST.

6. Use sources, numbers and statistics.

7. Don't present opinion as fact. If it's just an opinion admit it.

8. Keep smiling and stay positive even when disagreeing.

9. Make friends, not enemies. Praise the "silver linings" of opposing arguments.

10. Losing a few battles without losing your composure may help you win the war.

Chapter TWENTY-FOUR

LEAN AND SMACK

From error to error one discovers the entire truth.

Sigmund Freud

L ean and smack is perhaps the single most powerful tactic we have ever come across in our ongoing research on the best ways to engage an audience and motivate them to actively listen to a presentation. The power inherent in this tactic comes from the shock effect of letting people "lean" towards an "easy logic" answer or presumption, and then suddenly "smack" them with the harsh reality that the easy answer is not even close to the right answer. With "lean and smack" in the mix, people quickly learn they need to pay attention and think through issues carefully in order to avoid the jarring "smack." They learn that you have something to offer. They learn that you are worth listening to!

One method of setting a "lean and smack" into motion is to encourage people to chip in "top-of-mind," commonsense solutions. Once set in motion, the "lean and smack" tactic proceeds with a carefully-scripted series of five steps:

1. Record "top-of-mind" answers without showing any disapproval or criticism. Allow people to jump on the "group think"

bandwagon and travel down the wrong path that easy logic usually follows. This is the "lean."

2. Ask the group if the members want to see the results of implementing their solution. Then display the results and let them discover that their supposedly commonsense solution is hopelessly wrong. This is the "smack."

3. Smile and ask, "What happened?" Then allow everyone to be shocked or have a good laugh.

4. Seek out active listeners who have thought through the issue carefully but perhaps felt inhibited by others in the group. Encourage the active listeners to come forward and suggest different solutions.

5. Make it a point to compliment and/or reward those who have worked through the issue and thought beyond "top-of-mind" solutions.

A good "lean and smack" initially has the leader giving up control to the group, but by the end of the exercise the leader regains control by helping everyone discover for themselves that active listening is required and that easy logic and commonsense are not good enough to effectively solve the problem. Participants also find out they have something to learn from listening more carefully to each other. Furthermore, they learn to better appreciate the scope of the problem or task. And just as important, they learn the most serious downside of making a mistake in a situation like this is that everyone has some fun.

Sometimes talented leaders and communicators initially show some confusion over the value added by the "lean and smack" tactic. "Why would you want people to travel down the wrong line of reasoning just to have them discover their error later on?" "Aren't you wasting a lot of time?" "Give me some examples of what it is and how it works." "It may work for your situation, but not for mine."

Truth is, at least the "smack" of the "lean and smack" tactic has been around for a long time. One of the earliest examples comes from Britain when men were elevated to knighthood. The actual ceremony was not much like the ceremony we now see in the movies, Kings

Hollywood romanticizes the act of knighting. The real ceremony is not nearly so gentle!

would really whack the newly minted knight hard on the side of the head with the flat of the sword. What was the reason for the kingly head smack? To help the knight remember his newly made promises, duties, and responsibilities. And in most cases it worked very well.

Now, of course, even though we've all met some people that make us wish we could just walk up to them and smack them in the head with a sword, the flat of our hand or our briefcase, we can't actually do that to get them to remember what we say. On the other hand, we can smack them with their own sloppy thinking and cut through with a few powerful ideas and concepts. That works just as well and allows us to continue to stay in step with modern society.

It isn't unusual for people to remind us of a good "lean and smack" we gave them years after it happened. We believe in the tactic. We live by it. But if you happen to still be asking some questions, we understand. To clarify the nature of the tactic and why we like it we list several examples of "lean and smack" exercises and how we stumbled across each one. After you read the examples we invite you to try the tactic yourself. We feel that once you try the tactic and witness how people respond, you will understand why we are always on the lookout for new "lean and smack" opportunities.

Sometimes we simply bump into a "lean and smack" experience quite by accident. When we talk to business people about customer service we routinely show a video with Tom Peters talking about service quality. In the film we see how various businesses personify the different aspects of service quality. At one point we see a young woman receiving an award from her company for the outstanding work she has done during the previous year. As she receives the award she is overcome by emotion and begins to cry. Through her tears she thanks the company for making her feel like a part of the team and giving her a chance to make a positive impact on the business. Every time we show the film there are a few men in the audience who snicker and whisper to each other when we get to the "emotional woman" segment.

We had shown the training video several times and noticed the snicker element in our management audiences, when it finally occurred to us what we could do to make the management lessons cut through the wise-guy attitude of some of the viewers. We determined that the "emotional woman" segment would be a perfect "lean and smack" opportunity.

To set the "lean and smack" in motion we started showing the film, followed with a discussion in which we probed the group about their reactions to the film. In particular, we asked about the emotional segment, saying with a broad smile, "What did you think about the young women crying when she received her award?" Several men would always say that they were surprised how such a trivial award could be so important.

The young women in the group usually just sat back without making a comment, but we could tell that they were listening carefully to every word. Finally, the consensus was that the woman awardee was overly emotional and that no one should feel so strongly about their work. We nod our head with understanding, then lean in and say, "Now honestly, wouldn't all of us want to work for a company that could have that sort of positive impact on our own lives?" "What sort of responsibility do managers have to help employees gain skills and experiences that serve them off the job as well as on the job?" "Employees won't start providing high-quality customer service for the company until they feel the company is providing high-quality experiences for them." "When we run a company we are building more than a business; we are building people."

After the film and following discussion, presented in a congenial but still carefully planned "lean and smack" way, the people in the group have always eagerly expressed their appreciation for the lesson. In fact, one young lady was so moved by the experience that she later sent us a thank you note with a poem that expressed a senti-

ment similar to the presentation. "When we build a business," the poem says, "we should build people along with it."

We also find "lean and smack" opportunities when we make presentations about past experiences. One of the best stories we have for convincing people to do in-depth thinking and research comes from work with the American Plastics Council (APC) that we described in Chapter 1. Going on ten years now, APC has run a very successful public issue advertising campaign. As the ad campaign was being developed, plastics manufacturers like DuPont, Eastman Chemical and Dow Chemical faced decreasing demand for plastic products and packaging. At the same time the industry as a whole faced growing pressure from state lawmakers to ban or severely cut back on the use of plastics. Critics pointed out recycling problems, waste of energy resources, and the general negative impact of plastics upon the environment as reasons for reducing its use or in some cases abandoning it altogether.

We use the story to show why we need in-depth advertising research to deal with competition and public pressure. We set the "lean and smack" in motion by first saying that the APC ad campaign had been very successful. Next we give everyone a challenge to figure out an advertising message that will solve the plastics industry's problems with consumers, special interest groups and state lawmakers. Unknown to the audience, however, was that the APC advertising campaign was initially unsuccessful. Millions of dollars had been spent just to produce very modest positive changes in some areas, while in some cases noticeable declines were seen in public attitudes regarding plastics and the entire plastics industry.

Once we pose the problem, that is, how we should use advertising to improve public attitudes toward plastic, we ask for answers. Predictably, people begin by giving us "top-of-mind" commonsense answers, like stressing recycling plastic waste; they describe how it benefits the environment, etc., although these answers are entirely wrong, based on extensive research of which they are unaware. Once we gather their responses, we then compare their solutions to the initial flight of the plastic industry's television ads. People are always proud to see that their recommendations match the first round of APC ads almost perfectly. Everyone smiles and congratulates themselves on their victory. We play along, saying, "Wow!" "You hit the solution right on the nose and with only a few minutes of effort." "You are a gifted group of people!" This, of course, is the "lean."

At this point we ask if anyone would like to see the survey results that were gathered to track the effectiveness of the APC campaign. We hear a confident "yes" and so we put up the transparencies of charts and tables showing public attitude scores before and after the initial campaign. We ask what the numbers are saying about the actual effectiveness of the ads. Then there is a long silence. A hesitant voice from the group says, "It didn't work . . . the numbers aren't getting any better." Bingo. This is the "smack," delivered by a member of the audience, which is the best way to hit them with the reality. Now we have everyone's attention. Everyone is listening and thinking. We then discuss the issue until we find a solution based on an out-of-the box marketing perspective and some additional research data which we willingly provide. The validity of the new solution is confirmed when the second flight of ads is shown. The new ads were very successful and subsequent tracking results showed significant positive change in public attitude and behavior. The Lean and Smack efficiently cuts through sloppy thinking and knee-jerk reactions and pulls the group together to start actively thinking in new and productive ways about what they are hearing.

The key to making a "lean and smack" work is "confidence" on the part of the leader. If the leader can give up some personal control at the start and allow people to follow their own path, while asking questions that keep the path going in the desired direction for the desired results, it's an exciting and outstanding way of building team spirit and helping employees discover and use their intelligence and imaginations productively. When managers first use the tactic it is usually hard for them not to wince when members of the group suggest superficial "top of mind" solutions. Of course, wincing is not allowed or the effect will be spoiled. The big payoff, however, is proving to the people in your organization the value of actively listening. That alone will spur them on to learn for themselves how to think through an issue, rather than falling back on "pat answers" or allowing someone else to do all their thinking for them. The Lean and Smack tactic makes people better listeners, stronger thinkers and more engaged, more effective employees in any kind of workplace.

Part FIVE

Empowering the Love Group

Part FIVE

Empowering the Love Group

Winning over is the prescription for working with the Love Group. It is an approach to working with cooperative people that gets them to love the messenger and the message enough to put forth their best efforts. "Winning over" can be easier than we might first think.

Perhaps you recall Mark Twain's storybook hero, Tom Sawyer. His Aunt Polly wants to spoil his day by having him whitewash her fence. He has made plans to play, but has no choice but to work. Then he comes up with a "big idea." Why not have his friends do the work for him! He will have to help them see (i.e. persuade them) that whitewashing Aunt Polly's fence is a privilege, something that only a talented and committed person should be allowed to do.

But that won't be hard. He will just say how important it is to do the whitewashing just right, followed by giving up the brush reluctantly, and then only after making a good trade! He gets an apple from Ben Rogers, a kite from Billy Fisher, and from Johnny Miller a dead rat with a string attached to swing it with. Tom also picks up twelve marbles, six firecrackers, a tin soldier, a brass doorknob and so on, hour after hour. But the material treasures aren't that important to Tom. He can trade those back again. The real prizes are the three beautiful coats of whitewash on the fence, the astonished look on Aunt Polly's face and the great time he had with all his friends.

How did Tom do that? We can be pretty sure after thinking about that story years from then, Tom's bedazzled friends would still be

Used with permission © The Norman Rockwell Licensing Company

Multiply the Love

Energize your organization by calling the Love Group into action. Empower your employees to do difficult and tedious things by helping them feel the love!

wondering how they managed to get talked into doing Tom's chore for him. So here we are in a far more sophisticated and complicated world of persuasion and manipulation, and we're still thinking about barefooted little Tom and wondering, as we enter the Board Room with our presentation, or stand down on the work floor, how can we do what he did? How can we get large groups of people to do difficult and tedious things, have them thank us for the privilege and build strong friendships and alliances for the future? Exceptional leaders perform these modern-day miracles on a regular basis. How? Not by pushing and manipulating, but by dreaming up unique and friendly ways to empower the Love Group. By "empowering" we mean giving the Love Group the tools, confidence, and loving support they need to succeed in their own part of the task so that they can become our enthusiastic partners in leading the organization to success.

Chapter TWENTY-FIVE

WHO'S YOUR LOVE GROUP

Nothing takes the taste out of peanut butter
quite like unrequited love.

Charles M. Schulz

Before we can empower the Love Group, we first must figure out who they are. It can be more difficult to spot this group than it seems. For example, in the previous section, we introduced four categories of employees: foxes, kittens, puppies and tigers.

In our corporate training seminars, before we describe the four types of employees to managers, we ask them to name some of their most favorite and least favorite employees. Managers usually name kittens (low productivity and low service quality employees), as their most favorite, and tigers (high productivity and high service quality employees), as their least favorite. Foxes and puppies often go unnoticed. An odd result, but perhaps it is says something important about a manager's mindset.

So what is the truth? Are managers loving their Love Group or is their love unrequited? Our research with hundreds of employees at one Fortune 100 company indicated that 60% of tigers were classified in the Love Group. Whereas only 15% of kittens were in the Love Group and as a whole feel very untrusting about their supervisors and managers. Puppies were concentrated in the Hate Group. Foxes were evenly dispersed across all three groups.

Who's really in your Love Group?

	Hate Group	Swing Group		Love Group
		Untrusting	Bored	
Tigers	30%	---	10%	60%
Kittens	15%	50%	20%	15%
Foxes	30%	30%	10%	30%
Puppies	60%	---	10%	30%

The clustering of these numbers automatically raises several questions. Why does this company's managers believe that kittens and not tigers are in their Love Group when most kittens feel either untrusting or bored? Not all the tigers are in the Love Group, so has management done something to alienate them? Where did all those Hate Group employees come from? Certainly, we did not hire a Hate Group! Exploring these questions, we arrive at three axioms outlining points a leader should think about when working with the Love Group and when trying to understand the migration of employees from one group to another.

AXIOM # 1: THE LOVE GROUP IS NOT A PERPETUAL MOTION MACHINE

The Law of Conservation and the Law of Entropy currently are considered to be the two most important laws in the whole body of science. The Law of Conservation says that energy can be changed from one form to another, but cannot be destroyed. The Law of Conservation caused a big stir among industrial tycoons and basement inventors. Fortunes were spent trying to build a perpetual motion machine. The idea, of course, was to have a machine run forever by consuming its own exhaust. Countless brilliant designs were worked out on paper, the whole idea being that a perpetual motion machine, once it was put into motion, would produce its own energy and eliminate the need for any energy produced by steam, coal, oil, etc. Trouble is, the idea just doesn't work. This is because of the Law of Entropy, which says that in all energy exchanges, if no new energy enters the machine, the machine will eventually run down and stop because some energy is dissipated as heat.

That doesn't stop inventors with an unclear concept of both laws, and that doesn't stop some managers from continuing to act as though the Love Group in their organization is a perpetual motion machine, needing nothing and not losing any heat over time. However, these human dynamos will also run down and eventually grind to a halt just like every perpetual motion machine ever built, unless the manager expends significant energy now and then to wind them up again, like a spring-driven clock. The Law of Entropy demands that the Love Group receive periodic injections of energy to maintain their confidence, sense of direction, and high level of performance. Said another way, the Love Group requires a lot of management attention. The members of that group hate being ignored. They hate being taken for granted. They insist on getting your attention and conse-

quently can get under your skin. Tigers can be annoying. On the other hand, kittens are quiet and need very little to be happy. Therefore, why should the manager give so much attention and effort to the tigers? Answer: Tigers get the job done quickly and professionally, but if they are ignored the manager can expect an inevitable loss of energy in the performances of their jobs. Their potential energy or passion for work gradually degrades to match the results expected from a less committed, lower-quality employee. One who was once a great employee declines, or even worse, moves into the Hate Group. The productive heat is gone! All employees require our efforts, time, and skills and this is especially true for our most productive and conscientious employees.

We have seen managers spend a lot of their time and efforts focusing on their Hate Group. While such efforts are notable, they are somewhat misplaced. The Love Group needs at least an equal amount of attention. They tend to be the forgotten employees, regardless of the size of the total employee base or the type of work being done. You, as a Plus-One leader, should keep this in mind by categorizing the employees who take up most of your time before and after a meeting. Who frequently stops by your office to ask you twenty questions? Who has the enthusiasm to think outside the box when companies usually prefer inside the box thinking? The answer to these questions: members of your Love Group. We understand why leaders want to limit their time and effort with this group, because they aren't causing problems, but such thinking may be wide of the mark. Effective leaders continue to pump energy into their Love Groups because when things really get tough the Love Group has the ability to pull your bacon out of the fire!

AXIOM # 2: THE FORCE HAS A DUALISTIC NATURE

The popular Star Wars films center around two Jedi Knights, Anakin Skywalker and Luke Skywalker, who both possess a unique ability to tap into the Force. Their Master, Obi-Wan Kenobi, is responsible for teaching both students the ways of the Force. Obi-Wan Kenobi describes the Force as "An energy field created by all living things. It surrounds us, penetrates us, and binds the galaxy together." While both Luke and Anakin can wield the Force, they eventually end up tapping into different sides of it: Luke goes for the light side and Anakin takes the dark side. The light side of this mythic Force derives its energy from goodness, kindness, and belief in the genuine welfare of mankind. The dark side of the Force derives its strength from fear, hatred, and through the quest for power. While the plot of the movie infers that the dark side of the Force is more powerful, we find in the end that neither the dark side nor the light side of the Force is stronger than the other. They are in a sense dualistic or merely opposites in a continuum where balance is being sought.

Let's take that concept off the movie screen and project it magically into our suit and tie world of leadership. We might say that when someone loses balance and leans towards the dark side of the Force, there is a long-term inherent disadvantage to that person. For example, all of us are familiar with fictional accounts, and many of us have memories of real situations, where an individual believes he or she is superior to others. What happens to them? In most cases, both in fiction and in real life, their overconfidence eventually leads to their downfall. We have already highlighted the negative consequences that occur when leaders place themselves on the pedestal. Success often sows the seeds of failure.

There is a great personal value in understanding the parallels between the dualistic nature of the Force and everyday leadership. Some employees derive their motivation to work by focusing on the light side of the "Force." These employees feed off the positive vibes that come from a competent leader, the kindness of coworkers trying to do the right thing, and are deeply committed to the genuine welfare of the company. Other employees work hard by drawing from the powers of the dark side. Fear of being fired, seeking revenge, and the desire to have power over their colleagues and leaders motivate these employees. Unfortunately, those somewhat less-than-noble goals tend to draw them into the realm of the dark side. Interestingly, both types of employees have the motivation to do exceptional work. Both Love Group and Hate Group employees are generally productive, innovative and effective. Thus, we must look at the Hate Group and the Love Group as having equal energy for performing the work. The only difference between the two groups (other than the obvious: the Love Group wants to give you cookies and the Hate Group wants to poison those cookies) is the nature of their motivation. We must never destroy an individual's energy to work inside a company. If we do, we end up with more employees in the Swing Group-having little or no passion for their job. Their force is not captured in the company but is derived from activities outside the firm. We have stated frequently in this book that Hate Group members are not to be despised, punished, or looked down on. Such actions by leaders only fuel their dark side. Thank goodness they have that mythical Force to work—they are just struggling for balance, moving from the dark side of the Force to the light side of the continuum. Celebrate the whole continuum of the Force and learn to draw on it. We will learn in later chapters how leaders can cultivate and help employees see the advantages of the light side and find the right motives and orientations for work.

AXIOM # 3: MANAGERS CAUSE EMPLOYEE MIGRATION

We are often asked the million-dollar question, "where do the Love, Swing and Hate Groups come from? Were they just born that way? Is it like Darwinism, everyone starts out as a Love Group employee and eventually evolves into a member of the Hate Group? Do companies create their own Hate Groups or are these just a simple and inescapable fact of corporate biology?" The answers to these questions are complicated. However, empirical research suggests the root cause is most likely the behavior of the frontline manager, supervisor, or top executive. In other words, look in the mirror and you might just see the answer to the million-dollar question.

Over the years we have observed a few employees who migrate to and from different groups. Let's begin by addressing the central ebb and flow of employee migration. Continuing with the ideas discussed above in axioms 1 and 2, the dominant migration of employees from one group to another is Love Group employees turning to the dark side, i.e., joining the Hate Group. These migrants can be tigers or puppies. We shouldn't be surprised. After all, both employee groups have the Force but something happened in the company to disrupt the energy. Our research suggests turning employees to the dark side is the most common pathway because leaders have the opportunity to do so many harmful and thoughtless things that cause this migration to occur. We often play a game in executive seminars where managers are asked to think of all the ways they turn Love Group employees into members of the Hate Group. At first, everyone is usually very silent until we prime the pump. "Okay, how about the fact that we sometimes ignore their questions or don't have the time to meet with them." Of course any executive can relate to this experience. After a few minutes, our blackboard is full of reasons why good employees go to the dark side. A few of the central causes are listed below. Can you relate to any of them?

HOW GOOD EMPLOYEES TURN TO DARK SIDE

- Frustrations in dealing with an incompetent boss
- Trying to meet conflicting demands of various departments
- Not having enough help and equipment to accomplish tasks
- Dealing with people who fail to deliver as promised
- Having to sometimes stretch the truth
- Feeling that top management's decisions are sometimes unfair
- Not having the authority to do what is required
- Getting little support from leaders
- Having a boss that doesn't recognize contributions or abilities
- Having a boss who favors some employees over others
- Having a boss who will not go to bat for employees
- Feeling detached or left in the dark by management

Keep them in the dark; send them to the dark side

While we could go on for several pages outlining the problems that destroy the enthusiasm of a good employee, suffice it to say that many things managers do or say can turn good employees to the dark side of the Force. Perhaps the most insightful comment we heard while covering this topic was from a manager who has been dealing with a unique group of personalities for over 25 years. She said, "One thing I have learned about leadership is if you keep people in the dark, you turn them to the dark." In essence, when we neglect the insights, suggestions, questions and contributions of talented employees, we not only limit our potential as leaders, but we frequently turn such employees to the dark side.   When they have been neglected and under-valued, they may very well become demanding, confrontational and opinionated. This is unfortunate. There is another way.

Ebb and flow of employee migration

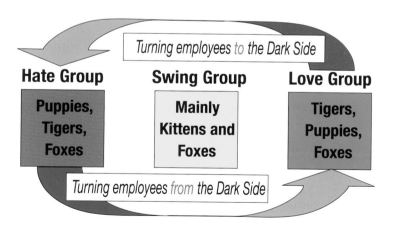

The second ebb and flow of the model is turning Hate Group employees from the dark side to the light side, i.e., into your Love Group. While this can happen, it is difficult to do and certainly does

"C'mon, guys. Give me a hint. Was it something I said?
Something I didn't say? Or was it the time I
raided your retirement fund?"

© BYU Academic Publishing

not happen by accident or luck. Turning employees from the dark side requires exceptional leadership skills and an appropriate mind-set that was apparently even beyond the abilities of the Jedi who were training Anakin. We must find ways to bring a person out of the dark by shining a bright light on their achievements and contributions. We must find ways to keep them "in the loop" and treat them as equals and not outsiders.

Using tactics discussed in Part 6, such as the Boomerang Effect, as well as tactics already covered in Part 3 such as Playing Along and knowing how to Explore tough issues, become paramount to your success in turning people away from the dark side.

Chapter TWENTY-SIX

PAINT THE TARGET AND SHOW HOW TO HIT IT

To be simple is to be great.

Ralph Waldo Emerson

Years ago one of our friends got a summer internship in the finance department at a leading pharmaceutical firm. He was ambitious and eager to prove himself. He asked for a tough assignment and got one. His task was to figure out the financial details for several merger and acquisition moves that the company was considering at the time. He wasn't given any guidance. He wasn't pointed in any particular direction. After all, he came from a top-tier graduate business program. Four weeks into the summer, totally frustrated that he couldn't make any headway on the problem or find people that would help him with the problem he returned to his supervisor. "How are you doing on the project," the supervisor asked. "I really haven't been able to make much progress," our friend answered. "Can you point me in the right direction?" The supervisor frowned and quipped, "I am sorry, that's not the full credit answer!" The next day, our friend was reassigned to the marketing department for the rest of the summer. Needless to say, he wasn't pleased with his experience at that company and actually went on to work at one of the country's top investment firms after graduation.

The Love Group wants to do it right

Have you ever got an assignment at work with a handful of general objectives or tasks, but no guidance? Like our friend, did you feel somewhat frustrated because you didn't know what set of small questions to ask in order to answer the big questions? Did you have to fall back on common sense or shoot-from-the-hip because you couldn't figure out when and where to use the appropriate procedures or tools? Have you ever looked at a solution someone has given you, scratched your head, and asked yourself how they ever came up with the answer? Have you ever taken an assignment in which you've felt that in order to do well with it you would have needed ten years experience working with it? Have you ever gotten out of a planning meeting just to look back at your notes a couple of hours later and wonder to yourself what you learned or what might be the next step?

For all of the reasons listed above, we have observed that many people, especially motivated people, want organizational tools that help them collect their thoughts, grasp thinking processes, and outline key steps, to help them feel confident when starting an assignment. If you want a team to do their best, here is some simple advice. Paint the target and show how to hit it. This is particularly true for motivating the Love Group. No doubt they have great potential, but want to perform so well, so flawlessly, they can "freeze up" unless they are shown exactly how to perform. In today's busy world it takes tremendous patience to become a really thorough manager, ahead of the curve in project solution, employee guidance and group maintenance, but to help develop the Love Group into future stars the great manager needs to make it a habit to outline work assignments step-by-step. When you are called upon to ask people to do a new set of tasks we recommend you paint the target big enough to satisfy everybody by using the following steps:

1. Outline the big questions within a work assignment.

2. Discuss the small questions to ask in order to answer the big questions.

3. Suggest the procedures and/or tools that would be most helpful in addressing each question.

4. Provide a detailed reporting format that includes how much effort should be devoted to each issue, in terms of hours or "page space."

5. Assign simple +/− importance values to each step in the process to help people learn the relative effort needed for each activity.

How should I cook that burger?

A recent survey of American businesses revealed that even in mundane job settings like the fast food industry, well over half of all employees say they do not clearly understand how to do their jobs correctly. In fact, in all the areas of business that we have researched, from hourly customer service representatives to business professionals, lack of adequate training is the most common complaint. Yet, as we travel around the nation to talk with managers, we have noticed that this issue creates a wide gulf between exceptional leaders and mere taskmasters. Many managers chafe at the suggestion of giving employees such detailed work plans. They say they want their teams to have the freedom to think for themselves. This surprises us because it has been our consistent finding throughout our life that **employee groups do a better job of thinking through a problem**

when they have a framework for thinking. And equally important, employee groups also begin to develop personal styles for collecting their thoughts and following through. Every great artist, composer, athlete, and scholar first learns the fundamentals. Great performances start with great coaches. We like to say that learning bits of information without a framework or process to tie the bits together is like trying to hold a carton of milk together without the carton.

In our research we find that exceptional leaders leap way ahead of their counterparts in helping people get organized. Once we were talking to a group of young men about ethics and posed a particularly tough dilemma for the group to consider. When we asked for solutions only one young man held up his hand. As he gave his solution and explained the thinking that went into it, the rest of the group sat back feeling a little stunned. Afterward we couldn't help but wonder how the young man had handled the problem so well? So we asked him if he'd reveal his secret. "Sure," he said, "the big sheet." We asked, "The big sheet, what's that?" "Well, I don't have it with me, but several years ago one of my Boy Scout leaders outlined things to think about when dealing with these sorts of problems and gave it to us on a big sheet of paper...we all started calling it the big sheet." We were impressed with how the "big sheet" gave a broad view as well as tremendous staying power to what the young man had learned several years earlier.

Plus-One leaders don't expect that people should always have to learn to think through tough problems on their own. They want to provide a rainbow that employees can ride to their own pot of gold. In contrast, we often wonder why is it that so many supervisors and managers expect people to somehow become critical thinkers and great performers without ever giving them examples of different ways to think critically or patterns of great performance! We just don't buy the argument that detailed assignments and step-by-step processes inhibit learning and creativity. Our experience shows that most "thinking paradigms" and "performance templates" contain enough flexibility and slack to let people arrive at their own conclusions in their own ways. From what we've seen, the best leaders will teach many processes, but impose very few "pat answers." If you want

Provide the Rainbow

Plus-One leaders provide their employees with a rainbow that they can ride to their own pot of gold.

Used with permission. © photos.com

to make a lasting impact, give people an interconnected thinking system and activity plans to draw upon when they address the big issues.

Build a toolkit

Many managers and supervisors like the idea of a "toolkit" to help them build their employee groups's thinking and working skills. However, they often are reluctant to create a unique and memorable language to make such a toolkit fun and worth learning. In fact, some of our colleagues become so annoyed by the simple language we have developed over time to use in our corporate training toolkits that from time to time they mumble under their breath that we are "trivializing" serious problems. Fact is, people remember better when they are having fun. It reminds us of the young men in The Church of Jesus Christ of Latter-day Saints who work as missionaries while living overseas and have to learn to speak a foreign language. It is always easy for them to learn slang words or phrases that are part English and part foreign language. While learning the real language, they also have fun creating a new language that only fellow missionaries can understand.

Unfavorable reactions to any suggestion that the leader should expend time and effort to build a fun and engaging "toolkit" are very similar to those unfavorable reactions we hear about using the Be Like Columbo tactic described in Part 1 of this book.

Managers fear they will lose the respect of their workers by inventing fun on-the-job language, introducing games into the work place, and using self-effacing humor. We don't buy it. In our experience having a fun and energetic personality is an important management asset. Fun concepts, memorable language, and down-to-earth leaders always make people stand up and cheer. Leaders we admire find simple ways to make their points without being simpleminded.

Chapter TWENTY-SEVEN

FIRST IN LAST OUT (FILO)

If I have ever made any valuable discoveries, it has been owing more to patient attention, than to any other talent.

Sir Isaac Newton

The Love Group wants time and attention. Arriving early and leaving late from team meetings provide perfect opportunities for the Love Group to show their interest, appreciation, and find out what they can do to contribute. At first blush, some managers think the tactic is pretty pompous - providing extra time for people to interact so they can enjoy your company and take pleasure in being part of your Love Group! On the surface, it does appear pompous, but the good news is that it works remarkably well for any manager who is willing to sacrifice the required personal time and attention. It is one of those simple tactics that seems to "cover a lot of management sins."

One manager reported that after he learned about the tactic, he decided to go back to the office after the normal 9-to-5 workday and spend some time with people working the night shift. First, he said, they were amazed to see a manager come back to look in on them and then doubly so because he brought along some fast food sandwiches to share with them. Even though he later admitted he felt like a "politician buying votes with roast beef sandwiches," he was able to dispel some rumors regarding a change in compensation, address questions about the company's business model and give the workers a heads-up regarding what to expect in the coming months in terms of sales and other goals. The manager recalled that through stopping by the office at 9:30 pm that one evening he was instantly accepted by the night crew. They now come to him to ask questions about where the business is heading and how they can best contribute. He feels he has even been able to turn some Swing Group employees into the Love Group.

Give love a chance

Another manager recalled that the FILO tactic surprised him. Rushing from one meeting to the next, he had completely ignored the opportunity to talk with employees before and after meetings. It was like he was the movie character Shrek—a kindly, but single-minded ogre moving from one task to another, trying to ignore the happy little donkey eager to help and be his friend. He was a victim of management's feared Shrek Syndrome, i.e., last person to arrive, first person to leave.

Shrek. © Dreamworks Animation

"Not now, Miss Smith. I'm busy lending a listening ear."

© BYU Academic Publishing

His first FILO experience was a real eye opener. He arrived five minutes early for a meeting and no one else showed up until ten minutes later! He realized that he had trained everyone to be late. He started the meeting by apologizing for always being late in the past and saying that in the future he would try to arrive a few minutes early. In addition, rather than running directly back to his office after the meeting, he lingered for a few minutes. He was glad he did because quite unexpectedly he was able to address some serious questions from a design engineer that resulted in improving scheduling, resource use and vendor selection.

All good relationships take time

It is easy to see the Love Group as a nuisance—just a bunch of people who demand time and attention that we don't have to give. However, we are amazed by the number of times managers are able to address serious issues, build trusting relationships, and improve employee performance by simply showing up a little early, staying a little late and lending a listening ear. Management magic often happens at the margins that separate our day-to-day activities. FILO is more, much more, than managing by walking around. Like the Greek word "philo," it is a kinship we feel and a commitment we make to give patient attention to those who want to contribute, who want to sacrifice, and who want to be our friend. A Plus-One leader will practice being accessible, not all day long (because that will never get anything else done), but at carefully selected times that can be built into the whole management schedule.

IDEAS FOR USING THE FILO TACTIC

1. Arrive for business meetings five minutes early and be ready to stay ten to fifteen minutes after the meeting is officially over.

2. Show up before or after normal work hours to see who is there and bring a surprise like a bag full of hot sandwiches.

3. Invite employees to an informal gathering, like a down-home barbeque.

Chapter TWENTY-EIGHT

JUMP ON THEIR BANDWAGON

Everyone takes the limits of their own field of vision for the limits of the world.

Arthur Schopenhauer

The need for vision in business and community leadership is not a new idea, but for some people, adopting and promoting the vision of those being led is a radical new idea. We have to admit that we only stumbled on the real importance of this leadership tactic when we were making a presentation about some marketing concepts and tools to an energetic young business team just a few years ago. Early on during every presentation of this particular seminar, it is common for one or both of us to be challenged by a financial manager, engineer, or accountant, i.e., someone who sees marketing as being manipulative, "smoke and mirrors," a necessary evil, or at most, just plain "common sense."

This time around it was a financial manager who spoke up and asked us, "I can't figure out why I should take the time to sit through all this stuff on marketing. Isn't it all just common sense? Since my boss has already paid for me to be here, please tell me that you have a good answer!" After pausing and searching a moment for what to say we replied, "Because marketing can make you a hero in your company if you do it well and surprisingly, there aren't that many people who ever learn to do it well."

We then went on to relate a true story about a young man named Sean who worked in the finance department of a large computer networking company. About a year earlier his CEO called an important meeting to discuss market conditions and strategies for increasing profit and market share. Having recently gone through our marketing seminar, Sean had asked some sharply focused questions in the meeting that impressed top management.

The next day, Sean was shocked to find out he had been promoted to the corporate marketing group and would receive a large pay raise. Management explained to him that the company desperately needed people like him with good marketing skills who had a well-rounded perspective regarding their business. Sean understood that marketing is all about asking the right questions, and that in this seminar, we would teach them the questions that lead companies in the right direction to solve profitability, market share and market growth problems. After hearing Sean's story the financial manager sat back and thanked us for answering his question.

"To Sean, our Hero for the day!"

If an idea has legs, run with it

We never gave a second thought to how we answered the financial manager's question. We were simply relieved he was satisfied with the answer so we could continue going through our material. During the next several sessions, however, we were stunned at the impact that our story about Sean had on the entire business team. The group was highly motivated and worked hard. Every time we discussed a victory in our own consulting projects, everyone in the group would lean forward in their seats and with their eyes lit up ask, "Did you make the manager a hero?" Stunned, we realized that every person on the team, not just the financial manager, had bought into the vision of becoming a hero within their own company. It was one of those magical moments you never forget. Well, we know marketing, so we knew what to do. We quickly jumped on the bandwagon of their vision with an elaboration of Sean's story. When asked the "hero" question from then on, we always answered with assurance, "As a matter of fact, the manager developed one of the most successful products of the decade for his company. He was a hero."

The sad part is, as corporate leaders and trainers we usually tell "war stories" about our own experiences because deep down we want people to know how great we are—what we have accomplished. However, what people in these training meetings really want to know is how did our training materials make someone else a company hero, or even more importantly and to the point, how can we make each of our meeting attendees a hero? We have never forgotten that humbling lesson.

Giving people a focused and personally relevant vision of their own potential is one of the most powerful services we can possibly render as we play our multiple roles as consultants, negotiators, business managers and teachers. Leading with vision is a tactic that every one of us can quickly grasp and start using. When we select a particular vision, however, it is all too easy to focus only on ourselves and our own ideas. This, of course, can be counterproductive. Consequently, we recommend that managers not only develop their own personal vision, but also more importantly, identify and promote the vision of their Love Group. In other words, jump on their bandwagon. It takes humility. It takes good listening skills and patience. It takes courage. On the other hand, when it's done with care and for positive results, it can create tremendous energy within the organization.

Below are three steps for leading with vision by jumping on the Love Group's bandwagon.

STEPS FOR LEADING WITH VISION

1. Think beyond your immediate goals and objectives for a moment. Listen for energy from the Love Group. What are some reasons that doing, learning, or thinking the things the Love Group wants will have a positive impact on the lives of others? There must be a greater end result than just accomplishing an immediate task or learning some facts.

2. Select a vision, i.e., a combination of goals and outcomes, from the alternatives identified in the first step. Make sure to pick a vision that you and the organization can actually deliver on, given available resources in time, equipment, personnel, etc.

3. Think of ways to highlight that selected vision in a way people will find personally relevant. To really jump on the bandwagon and maintain a comfortable seat there, you must bring the vision to life.

Vision must be grounded in experience

To start winning over a group you've got to give them a good road map showing where you are taking them. Marking the road map with a big, painted target, an "X" to show where the group is going, gets people to think beyond the day-to-day tasks of the job. In the movie Dead Poet's Society, Mr. Keating (portrayed by Robin Williams) gives us a great example of "leading with vision." Before he even starts his first lecture he leads his students into the hallway where there is a glass case with dusty trophies and faded pictures of students long since forgotten. As the schoolboys line up in front of the trophy case, he tells the students that they may call him Mr. Keating, or—if they are slightly more daring, "Oh Captain my Captain." He then asks the boys to read aloud several verses of the poem, To Make Much of Time. The poem goes:

> Gather your rose buds while you may,
>
> old time is still a flying, and this same flower
>
> that smiles today, tomorrow will be dying.

Mr. Keating goes on to explain the Latin expression for this bit of verse is carpe diem, which translates to "seize the day." Having grabbed their attention, he asks them to glance at the faces of the young men of the past whose pictures hang in the trophy case. While they stare deeply into the faces of those young men, once much like them but now passed away, he takes advantage of the magical moment and whispers with a ghostly laboring voice, "Carpe diem, carpe diem! Seize the day, boys! Make your lives extraordinary."

Mr. Keating's first "lecture" is all about how he develops a shared vision for the class, i.e., a love for poetry and the need for living an extraordinary life by learning to think and act for yourself. He tells the young men in their next class, "I have a secret for you. We don't read and write poetry because it is cute. We read and write poetry because we are members of the human race and the human race is filled with passion. Medicine, law, business, engineering, these are noble pursuits and necessary to sustain life, but poetry, beauty, romance, love, these are what we live for."

Dead Poets Society. © Touchstone Pictures

Seize the day

Plus-One leaders provide a shared vision for employees to rally around and pursue with passion.

"I spent a lot of effort leading you with vision and instilling enthusiasm in your workday and Im thrilled now at the way you're responding, but—wait—we seem to be heading for the company dumpster."

© BYU Academic Publishing

Transcend the day-to-day

Leading with vision requires us to find a goal that transcends our day-to-day routines. Napoleon expressed the idea very well when he said, "A man does not have himself killed for a half-pence a day or for a petty distinction. You must speak to the soul in order to electrify him!" In a sense we are answering an unspoken question in the backs of our listeners' minds, "What can listening to you or doing what you want, do for me personally in my life?" "Beyond a lousy 15 cents an hour raise, an employee of the month award, or just working harder and staying later, what's in it for me?" "Convince me its worth it!"

Vision gives people a goal and the goal gives them the willingness to listen and the energy to apply what they hear—particularly when the vision is born out of their own work and life experiences. Listening with enough focus to actually hear takes a lot of effort. For most people, listening to a supervisor, manager, or even a college professor is not rewarding enough on its own to be an end into itself. Leading with vision creates a payoff worth the pain of listening and trying new things.

Chapter TWENTY-NINE

MAKE A MINI-ME

You can delegate authority, but not responsibility.

Stephen W. Comiskey

In almost any leadership text you can read about the importance of delegation or entrusting your authority to others. In 1530 Palsgrave, one of the first people to use this principle, wrote, "I delgate myne auctorite." While delegation is widely touted as a pinnacle of leadership for making your life easier, it is rarely understood and frequently abused. For example, if you tell a subordinate to maintain service quality by monitoring and correcting employee performance every Monday and Friday while you are in Europe and if there happens to be a holiday that falls on Monday and Friday, the employees will likely go a week without monitoring and service quality certainly will suffer. Yet the subordinate did exactly as told. Trouble is, as leaders, we want to delegate our responsibility, but not our authority.

Many managers delegate with phrases like, "if there is any trouble, immediately call my cell phone, or remember to fire any employee who does not meet the quota this month." In short, when we delegate responsibility and not authority we are not training employees to reach their full potential. We are not training employees to be leaders. We are simply providing employees with, "don't forget" post-it-notes. No real learning here or delegation. However, you do get to have fun with a lot of multicolor post-it-notes. We prefer yellow and teal.

Put delegation to bed

In our experience, delegation is so misunderstood and misused as to become an outdated activity that needs to be put to bed. We believe there is a much simpler tactic that supplants the need for delegation that we call, "Make a Mini-Me". The idea of making a Mini-Me was first introduced to the world in the 1997 comedy adventure movie, Austin Powers, The Spy Who Shagged Me. In the movie, Dr. Evil develops a time machine that allows him to go back in time to steal Austin Powers' mojo. In the beginning of the movie, Dr Evil is shown circling the globe in his cryonic state while his vile employees try to figure out what to do without him. Realizing the need for leadership, Dr Evil's employees secretly clone another Dr Evil. Well, actually, a clone 1/8 his size called, "Mini-Me". Thus, the idea of cloning a leader was born. We were immediately captivated with the idea.

Don't Be Afraid to Make a Mini-Me

Plus-One leaders train and mentor the Love Group into an army of Mini-Me's.

Austin Powers. © New Line Cinema

A story of Jack and Jill

Why would anyone want a Mini-Me? To understand just why, let's discuss two managers who both work at Mother Goose, Inc., a company that manufactures children's fables. Two of Goose's crack managers are named Jack and Jill. One weekend they went to the hills to fetch a little rest and recreation from their stressful jobs.

While Jack was climbing a particularly steep hill to fetch some refreshment, he fell down and hit his head on a sharp rock. Jill, seeing what happened ran to his side but unfortunately tripped, tumbling down on top of Jack and hit the same rock. When they both got up to trot home they felt dizzy and fainted. Fortunately for them, they were spotted and rushed to a nearby hospital. At the hospital, the doctor informed them that they both had suffered severe concussions and could not return to work for two weeks. After two weeks of nursing, Jack and Jill recovered, placed their belongings in a brown paper bag, and went back to work.

When Jack came back to the office he was immediately met by his supervisor who exclaimed, "It's chaos in here. Glad you're back because it has been a nightmare without you." The minute Jack stepped into his office he was inundated by his employees. "What are we going to do with the backlog of rhyming and writing? We're drowning here - nobody is putting this mess back together again!" You see, Jack's management style was to get employees to do some "hum de dum" and the occasional "la la la," but not give anyone a complete picture of what he was trying to accomplish.

He frequently placed post-it-notes on the desks of all his employees to keep them on track, but perhaps afraid of being outdone by the employees, he kept his considerable abilities and talents to himself. You might say he didn't want anyone to know or discover his secret sauce; the tactics, knowledge, and skills necessary to run the division. Such skills gave Jack power and allowed him to be recognized as one of the key managers that the company could not do without.   Jack sometimes let all the power go to his head. After he distributed the small and inconsequential assignments on brightly colored post-it-notes, he often leaned back in his chair and sighed, "This would be a great job if I didn't have to work so hard to get employees to cooperate - I guess if you really want something done right, you've got to do it yourself!"

When Jill returned to her job she experienced quite a different scene. As she met with her supervisor, he simply asked how she was feeling and thanked her for coming back to work so quickly. He suggested that a little vinegar might help her head heal up faster. When she stepped into her office, she found on her desk a number of post-it-notes from her subordinates telling her how much they appreciated her and that they had taken care of her duties while she was out and not to worry. There was no huge backlog of work, because one of her employees went the extra mile and kept her duties caught up during her absence. You see, Jill's management philosophy was, if you want something done right, train others to do it with you. She had taken the personal time to create a Mini-Jill. She understood that great companies need a queue of great leaders just waiting for the call to lead. Not threatened by her employees, she not only entrusted authority to others but also developed, trained and shared her secret sauce, thereby building a cadre of employees who were ready to take her place. Jill's division is a well-run business unit capable of moving to infinity and beyond even when the boss is away. Jill understood the secret of mini-me. If you turn your employees into stars, you make your own star shine brighter!

Military and the Mini-Me

The military understands the importance of making regiments of Mini-Me's, even though they don't talk about it using the same terms. In the heat of battle, if a leader is injured or proves to be ineffective, the Army can't allow a chaotic gap in leadership, which would

**Train Your
Next Worf.**

A manager, like a lieutenant is a place holder. Train other capable people to step into your management shoes.

put the fighting unit in even greater danger, as well as preventing it from successfully completing its mission. In such a situation, experienced backups are absolutely essential. This particular mindset is reflected in the military term lieutenant—the rank given to young military officers. The term lieutenant comes from the French words "lieu" meaning "place" and "tenant" meaning "holding". Taken literally, a lieutenant is only a placeholder until another leader is called up to take his position.

As leaders in the workplace, we should think of ourselves as placeholders so that in the heat of competition, there is someone else standing behind us who is capable, in the event of any problem, of stepping in immediately to lead the charge. The Make a Mini-Me leadership tactic reinforces the notion that a manager is a placeholder; one who holds a position of responsibility and one who develops the skills, knowledge and tactics of his subordinates by delegating true authority to make decisions based on a thorough understanding of the big picture and what needs to be accomplished. In short, don't merely delegate responsibility. Be extraordinary and make a Mini-Me. If you are very daring, make several!

Chapter THIRTY

REWARD THEM BEFORE THEY BEG FOR REWARD

Too many have dispensed with generosity in order to practice charity.

Albert Camus

Management by exception is a growing trend in modern business because of the increasing complexity of our world. Managers use computer screens to carefully scrutinize personalized executive dashboards that point out problem areas - the exceptions - that need immediate attention.

By and large, management by exception focuses attention on the negative. Often lost in the shuffle is the Love Group that day in and day out flawlessly performs their job. Members of the Love Group don't complain when asked to do something extra, they provide a positive example for other workers, they spot what needs to be done and do it without prompting, they don't assume they already know everything, and they volunteer for new and difficult tasks others avoid.

In some organizations, the only time the Love Group is noticed is when they are gone, or when they are forced to beg for time off, a raise, or extra help. At that point, managers typically practice Scrooge-like charity, distributing miserly doles that require some extra effort or sacrifice in return. It is demoralizing. It is bad business. We must ask ourselves, are we responsible for turning yet another member of the Love Group to the dark side?

You Scrooge, Me Scrooge, We all Scrooge

Quoting from A Christmas Carol by Charles Dickens, we listen in on a conversation between Scrooge and his faithful clerk, Bob Cratchit:

"You'll want all day tomorrow, I suppose? said Scrooge. If quite convenient, sir. It's not convenient, said Scrooge, and it's not fair. If I was to stop half-a-crown for it, you'd think yourself ill-used, I'll be bound? The clerk smiled faintly. And yet, said Scrooge, you don't think me ill-used, when I pay a day's wages for no work. The clerk observed that it was only once a year. A poor excuse for picking a man's pocket every twenty-fifth of December! said Scrooge, buttoning his great-coat to the chin. But I suppose you must have the whole day. Be here all the earlier next morning. The clerk promised that he would; and Scrooge walked out with a growl."

It is surprising how many managers can come off as modern, 21st century Scrooges. Equally as surprising is the fact that people can vividly recall Scrooge-like experiences with their leaders for many years after they happen. One manager told us, "I remember working for a local not-for-profit organization when going through school many years ago. We knew there was no money for bonuses or other special compensation for doing a particularly good job, but considering who we were working for and the job we were doing we wanted the occasional kind word or thank you note. Unfortunately my manager, like many others, believed that thanking employees was not necessary. Now several years later, because of that experience, one thing I try to do as a manager is to make sure my employees do not go through what I went through." She then shared a personal story about asking one of her employees to come in and work on a Saturday in order to finish a project. She was thrilled when the employee cheerfully agreed right away to come in. To thank him, she surprised the employee by immediately handing over some movie tickets for him and his family. Then she was surprised at how pleased he was and how fast the good news traveled through the organization. During the next team briefing one of her team members eagerly asked when she could come in and work a Saturday.

I OUGHT TO CAUGHT YA

An "instant reward" program was put into practice several years ago by one of the best and hardest working CEOs with whom we've ever worked. He calls it the "caught ya" program. He introduced it to make sure company managers would be on the look out for the good efforts and performances of employees. At a minimum, once a month each member of the management team must find an exceptional employee to recognize and reward. The rewards are usually movie tickets, dinner certificates, or other kinds of gift certificates. Also, when giving out a "caught ya," the manager will write out a brief note to express appreciation, highlight a specific contribution, and encourage the employee to keep up the good work. Once a month all the production employees are brought together for an awards meeting. It always generates a lot of excitement. It provides a great opportunity to recognize individuals as well as the combined efforts of the company.

Recently, a "caught ya" was awarded to Allen and Solomon, two men working on the swing shift. During the shift, one of the large pieces of manufacturing equipment caught on fire. The two employees quickly got everyone out of the building, and then went to work putting out the fire while the fire department was in route. Because of their quick efforts, only thousands of dollars of damage was done rather than hundreds of thousands. But the story doesn't stop there. After they put the fire out, the men stayed late repairing the machinery so that when the day shift arrived at 6:00 am, the machinery was up and running.

We all love to be loved and when we are lucky enough to have it happen, we should never overlook it or take it for granted. It is a rare gift that deserves to be nurtured and cherished. But not only does it feel good, it is just good business. If employees don't feel that their passion for the job is acknowledged, they will begin to do only the

Energize them

Energize the Love Group by rewarding them before they beg for reward!

minimum work required, if that. Then watch how fast the company fills with foxes and kittens. All the tigers and puppies, people that put real passion into what they are doing, will go elsewhere for personal satisfaction and excitement in their work.

Searching for the thousand points of light

We wish it was simple to find examples of the tactic Reward Them Before They Beg for Reward. But frankly we don't hear many stories about it. Perhaps it is the company we keep or that people tend to have an easier time recalling experiences in which they've lost rewards rather than been surprised with rewards.

There are whole books dedicated to the topic, but we personally have seen many instances of grand disappointments. For example, the time when an enthusiastic new employee had to read through his daily batch of emails to discover he had won his organization's Employee of the Year award rather than being personally congratulated by company executives. Or consider how one employee must have felt when she worked day and night to ensure the success of a high profile project and then spent countless hours gathering together information about the project to submit the application and ultimately win a national award. Just to see another person not even remotely associated with the project step into the spotlight and accept the award. Then there is the management team that revolutionized their business and a tired, old industry, dramatically increased their profitability, and won Product of the Year honors from Fortune Magazine. Within a decade, the same management team was laid-off or forced into early retirement and eventually watched from the sidelines as their business was sold off to the highest bidder.

Amidst all the darkness, however, there are some points of light. We were thrilled to hear the story from a young woman about her six-teenth birthday. As a complete surprise her parents organized a birth-day party dance for her, inviting the whole community, and of course, all of the young men she liked the best were there, too. The parents wanted to thank their daughter for giving them sixteen wonderful years.

Then there is Cindy, a community leader with a tremendous heart. The morning after every activity they worked on, every mem-ber of her "activity team" received a thank you card with a small pres-ent on their doorstep. Just something simple and corny like "You're a Joy to Work With" bundled with an Almond Joy or "You're Support and Friendship is Worth a Million" combined with a 100 Grand Bar. Cindy even returned from a tour in the Holy Land with terracotta oil lamps for every woman she had worked with that year and attached the message "Knowing You Fills My Lamp with Oil."

Cindy understands something that many of us not-so-natural-born leaders apparently miss. That is, when you are a leader, you have a special opportunity to add to the light of the world if you answer the call of "caressme." A daughter, a close associate, an out-standing employee, really everyone needs to know in their heads and feel in their hearts that everything they do, every sacrifice they make is really worth it. Leaders, whether they realize it or not, are in the unique position to make these small miracles happen.

Please become expert at wielding the tactic Reward Them Before They Beg for Reward. It might be a kind note. It might be added training and authority. It might be a generous word, warm touch and proud look when presenting an award. We all love and respond to rewards and surprises of appreciation.

Part SIX

Surviving, Performing, Thriving

Part SIX

SURVIVING, PERFORMING, THRIVING

*L*es Choristes (The Chorus) is a remarkable film we believe every manager ought to see. Critics describe it as a "gentle French drama in which music teacher Clement Mathieu lands a job at boys' boarding school populated by delinquents and orphans and run by a martinet headmaster." The film and the boarding school, however, are anything but gentle. It is bound to strike a cord with anyone who has been faced with having to manage unmanageable people with senior management who is self absorbed, uncaring and sometimes cruel. For example, when Mathieu first arrives at the boarding school the headmaster first scolds him for arriving a few minutes late and then humiliates Mathieu as all of the staff and boys look on by insisting he address him only as headmaster. Things like this don't just happen in the movies. We knew a supervisor like this once. Thank goodness we didn't have to work for him. We followed his career at a company which was one of our clients, observing him and his business team for several years. We watched with interest as every single member of his team quit or transferred to another business within six months of coming on board with him. This manager took on the tough assignment of a team leader and made life unbearably tough for everyone around him.

What survivors can do

The Chorus begins with Mathieu feeling very unsure of himself. His lack of confidence is only reinforced by the harshness of the head-master. The headmaster's mantra is "action-reaction," i.e., if anyone steps out of line, slap him down. It rarely, if ever, seems to work the other way around. Performing well in the classroom is expected and not rewarded. Next, Mathieu is faced with the boys. They are unruly, uncooperative, and they can be dangerous. How can Mathieu survive in such a setting, let alone perform well or thrive? The answer to that question is what makes the film valuable and is what the critics—who may miss the most valuable point of this little gem of French cinema—all but gloss over. Mathieu has had a lot of hard knocks in life and he knows how to survive. When he walks into the classroom he sees that one of the boys has drawn a cartoonish sketch of him on the blackboard, while the other boys in the room loudly chant "chrome dome" in reference to Mathieu's bald head. The knee-jerk reaction in such a situation is to indignantly scold the boy, quickly erase the drawing, and then shout to quiet the classroom, the classic "action-reaction" plan so common in every schoolroom in the world. Mathieu, however, does something quite different. He steps back and admires the drawing and compliments the boy. Then he quiets and captures the attention of the class by making his own drawing of the boy. Mathieu knows the first two rules of survival. He adroitly moves himself from the center of the target by laughing at himself. He plays along by making a drawing of his own.

Using these two simple tactics gives Mathieu an opportunity to succeed where so many others had failed before. But it doesn't stop there. Next, he notices that one of the toughest boys loves music. Mathieu decides to encourage the boy, i.e., *Pai Ma Pi,* and then decides to introduce a few Surprise Piles for the boys by having them sing songs about their life in the boarding school. After all, Mathieu is a musician. He can engage the boys in something fun and play to his own strength at the same time. Mathieu survives, performs wonderfully, and thrives—and so do the boys. The film offers entertainment and interesting characters as well as an important lesson, easily digested to help managers in the corporate world or any other area where really exceptional leadership is critically needed, admired and rewarded.

THE LEADERSHIP TEMPLATE

Failing to prepare is preparing to fail.

Unknown

E ffective leadership rarely just happens. Observing how managers think about and verbally approach their work through role play exercises offers convincing evidence that most tough leadership situations require careful thought and preparation. Leaders, no matter how brilliant, insightful and personally charismatic they might be, still benefit from a template to help them think through their challenges and prepare ahead of time as much as possible to select the right tactics and exercises for what they want to accomplish.

The leadership template we have constructed below looks suspiciously like the outline of a classic Greek temple (see Leadership Template on the next page). This wasn't just a serendipitous accident. This template is our own Leadership Parthenon, and it can serve the thoughtful modern manager in ways the ancient Greeks could only guess at. The foundation for our temple-template is, of course, a believing mindset. Cultivating a believing mindset makes every leadership tactic work better and it can even compensate for the mistakes we are sure to commit. If we do not use a believing mindset as our own foundation as we approach our leadership responsibilities, we can only

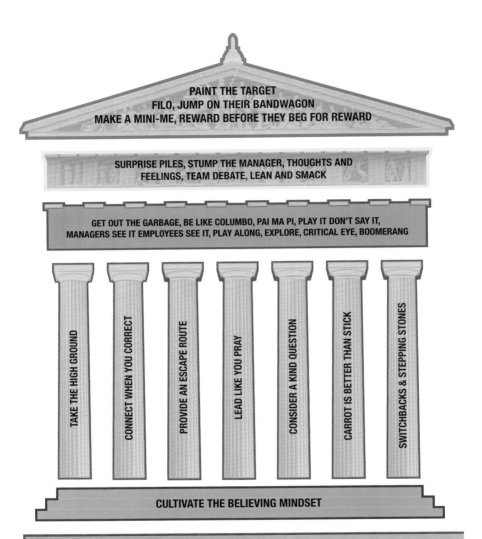

The Leadership Template

Our Leadership Parthenon can serve the thoughtful modern manager in ways the ancient Greeks could only guess at.

THE LEADERSHIP TEMPLATE

Failing to prepare is preparing to fail.

Unknown

Effective leadership rarely just happens. Observing how managers think about and verbally approach their work through role play exercises offers convincing evidence that most tough leadership situations require careful thought and preparation. Leaders, no matter how brilliant, insightful and personally charismatic they might be, still benefit from a template to help them think through their challenges and prepare ahead of time as much as possible to select the right tactics and exercises for what they want to accomplish.

The leadership template we have constructed below looks suspiciously like the outline of a classic Greek temple (see Leadership Template on the next page). This wasn't just a serendipitous accident. This template is our own Leadership Parthenon, and it can serve the thoughtful modern manager in ways the ancient Greeks could only guess at. The foundation for our temple-template is, of course, a believing mindset. Cultivating a believing mindset makes every leadership tactic work better and it can even compensate for the mistakes we are sure to commit. If we do not use a believing mindset as our own foundation as we approach our leadership responsibilities, we can only

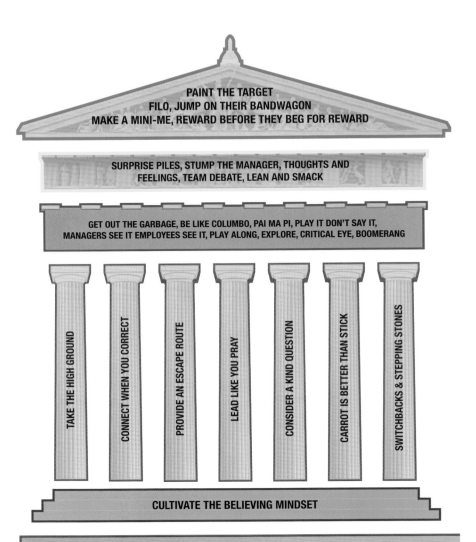

PAINT THE TARGET
FILO, JUMP ON THEIR BANDWAGON
MAKE A MINI-ME, REWARD BEFORE THEY BEG FOR REWARD

SURPRISE PILES, STUMP THE MANAGER, THOUGHTS AND
FEELINGS, TEAM DEBATE, LEAN AND SMACK

GET OUT THE GARBAGE, BE LIKE COLUMBO, PAI MA PI, PLAY IT DON'T SAY IT,
MANAGERS SEE IT EMPLOYEES SEE IT, PLAY ALONG, EXPLORE, CRITICAL EYE, BOOMERANG

TAKE THE HIGH GROUND

CONNECT WHEN YOU CORRECT

PROVIDE AN ESCAPE ROUTE

LEAD LIKE YOU PRAY

CONSIDER A KIND QUESTION

CARROT IS BETTER THAN STICK

SWITCHBACKS & STEPPING STONES

CULTIVATE THE BELIEVING MINDSET

I LIKE YOU, WANT TO GET TO KNOW YOU, BELIEVE YOU ARE VERY CAPABLE

The Leadership Template

Our Leadership Parthenon can serve the thoughtful modern manager in ways the ancient Greeks could only guess at.

expect to appear stiff, mechanical and perhaps even uncaring to those we are leading and working with.

Pillar principles

Each major leadership principle is represented by a vertical pillar and we use colors to easily identify the three "worker profiles" found within every work group. The pillars connect us with red tactics for the Hate Group, yellow tactics for the Swing Group, and green tactics for the Love Group. Principles are pillars because they are more than mere tactics or exercises. They are an extension of mindset.

When we have developed the right mindset, our spontaneous actions within the bounds of the seven principles will become second nature. If we sincerely believe in the capabilities of others, for instance, we will automatically attack the problem and not the person. We will find a kind, positive way to highlight and correct faults. We will provide ways for people to retain their self-respect even when they make mistakes.

We will thank people for what they have done *before* we ask them to do something new. We will ask others for help to meet a challenge, rather than telling others what to do, which would make the most exciting challenge just another chore. We will reward good choices rather than punish bad choices. After all, making a bad choice is punishment enough to a person who really wants to do the job right. We will create opportunities for our employees to succeed and take the time to celebrate their achievements.

That sounds like pretty simple stuff, but we are all human so it is important to remind ourselves daily to stand on that believing mindset foundation, look up at the pillars of those seven principles and test ourselves. Do we violate any of the principles when we interact with employees, friends, family? If so, we still haven't spent enough time standing on that believing mindset foundation. But what if we fail (and we will)? We shouldn't despair.

The Greek educator Socrates, whose own leadership template has been a model to follow for almost three millennia, observed, "The unexamined life is not worth living for man." From what we have observed, just knowing the test and then submitting oneself to regular examination makes all the difference between success and failure: Review, adjust and try again. We do our best. We forget something and fall on our face. We get up and smile. We'll do better next time!

The tactics to tackle first

Three groups of tactics complete our temple-template. Nearly half of the tactics are focused on the Hate Group. We have worked particularly hard to identify "red tactics" because we have seen Hate Group dynamics in action cause tremendous damage to businesses and managers. In fact, we feel that new managers must first learn to deal effectively with the Hate Group just to survive. Among the red tactics, the three to master first are Be like Columbo, Play Along—Move Along, and Explore. Adopting these tactics as our own has changed our lives and we feel confident that when they are understood and mastered they will change your life as a leader in ways that are both exciting and rewarding. They are the first line of defense against being intentionally humiliated and possibly ruined by an experienced Hate Grouper. Stay off the pedestal by using small doses of self-deprecating humor. When you or your ideas are attacked, accept the criticism in a good-natured way. You may even want to play up and exaggerate the criticism to make it look silly and absurd. If your assailants don't lighten up, look at their faces for clues (yes, you really can frequently read a person's motives by just studying their faces as they make their points) , then be brave and explore. Collect thoughts and opinions on both sides of the issue and reinforce the positive energy that comes out of such discussions.

The next two levels of tactics are directed at the Swing Group and Love Group. The "yellow tactics" are important for engaging the fence sitters, often the kittens of an organization who don't believe in themselves or their managers. In some organizations, kittens make up more than half of all employees. A business can't start performing to its potential *until* managers reach out and successfully motivate the Swing Group. Tactics like Surprise Piles and Thoughts and Feelings help the Swing Group develop trust in their managers. Tactics like Stump the Manager, Team Debate and Lean and Smack help the Swing Group come out of their shell and develop trust in themselves. At the pinnacle of our leadership temple-template stand the "green tactics." The green tactics reenergize the Love Group. Yes, the Love Group does take your special attention (your mother might call it "coddling"), but it's worth it to offer clear direction, sincere attention, support for their ideas and rewards for their performance. The members of this group will thrive and the results and positive feedback will make all your careful preparations in laying a good mindset foundation, followed by careful placement and raising of those seven principle pillars well worth the effort. In may ways, a vibrant, growing, and enthusiastic Love Group is the capstone of Plus-One leadership.

Chapter THIRTY-TWO

MINDING THE MINDFIELDS

> *Do not always expect good to happen, but do not let evil take you by surprise.*
>
> Czech Proverb

The first time we went to London and traveled the Tube, the London subway system, we were confused by the recording that played every time the train doors opened and closed. After struggling to understand the words through the English accent, we worked out that the recording was saying, "Mind the gap." Now what did that mean? We asked a local gentleman next to us in the subway, and he kindly pointed out the gap being warned about is a wide and deep drop off between the train and the tracks. We never even thought to look! We didn't know there was a danger, but evidently enough people had fallen into the gap to necessitate a recording to tell everyone to mind it. Every war has its minefields that can kill and maim the unwary, and every management position has its corporate "mindfields," which are in their own way dangerous to the unthinking or unprepared manager. A mindfield is something that happens or gets said over and over again that disturbs or angers people. Like when a math teacher says, "The answer is obvious," and it's only obvious if you spent four years at M.I.T. like your math teacher did, or a proud mother looks down at your drooling toddler and just has to say, "My two-year-old Jimmy already talks in full sentences and is reading at a third-grade level," implying strongly that in the case of your child, evolution works backwards.

Obviously, what a manager says to the workers on his team, and how he says it, are critical to maintaining both vital flow of information and team spirit. Very simple, but many managers don't realize that when they talk to ten, twenty, maybe a thousand employees, they're not talking to a bunch of bobbing heads, but to each individual. But what do managers say and do that really gets under the skin of employees? Leaders tend to develop lists, and everybody, managers and workers alike, love those top ten lists, whether it's the ten ugliest pets in the world or the ten most beautiful women or the ten most irritating leadership habits. So, during our training seminars we ask groups of managers to work in teams to assemble their own list of the top ten signs your boss is a schmuck. Here is the list we have compiled from our seminars.

TOP TEN SIGNS YOUR BOSS IS A SCHMUCK

#10 Withholds important information

#9 More interested in building an empire than building a successful business

#8 Plays favorites and ignores genuine contributions

#7 Constantly tells, but never asks

#6 Loves red tape and creates it all the time

#5 Micromanages every detail of my life

#4 Assigns meaningless tasks and tells me it will help my career

#3 Hypocrisy—always breaking their own rules

#2 Always the last in and first out from every meeting

#1 Taking personal credit for work done by their employees

We don't claim that this is the perfect list. We are confident, after years of being told about truly Olympian schmucks, our list could be much longer and include many disturbing, angering, *business-damaging* behaviors. However, even if the list skips over a couple of your all-time favorites, there is great value in this list. First, every time we do this exercise, teams spend a lot more time arguing over what should be included in the top ten than they do thinking up what to add to the list. Second, employees are watching and evaluating their managers all the time. This is particularly true of seasoned employees. When you don't return a smile, when you forget a name, when you lose your cool, somebody will notice it, remember it and talk at great length about it. And no matter what great things you have accomplished, prepare to slip back a few steps in the mindfield and start over to gain the respect and confidence caused by just one little misstep.

Know your own mindfields

As we've described above, stumbling in a mindfield can kill the positive momentum you are building as a leader. If you knew something would hurt you, wouldn't you want to avoid it? Management mindfields are dangerous. While much of what we are talking about in this leadership training material are strategies and tactics to learn well and store in some easily accessible place in your mind for quick recovery, it is a good idea to keep a tangible (i.e. printed) list of management mindfields on your desk where you will automatically scan it when you reach for the phone or move a chart. We believe this is just as important as keeping a list of leadership tactics at hand for quick reference.

Developing a customized list for each of your leadership venues is another good idea. Make sure your list has at least five entries. For example, if you are a mom or dad, list the things you say or do that aggravate your spouse or children. If you are a manager, list the things managers say or do that exasperate your employees. If you are a community leader, list the things leaders say or do that frustrate the members of your community. Paraphrasing an old quotation, to err is human, to forgive is not really human at all. It's best to avoid stomping through the mindfield in the first place, and it's best to avoid the big mistakes completely!

Chapter THIRTY-THREE

Please Don't Hate the Hate Group

But I say unto you, love your enemies, bless them that curse you, do good to them that hate you . . .

Matthew 5:44

We like to think about the Hate Group as having its own mascot among the gods of Greek mythology. That goddess is called (depending on which language is being used) Eris, Strife, or Discordia. According to an old Greek entertainer named Homer, this goddess is famous for starting the Trojan War by tossing a golden apple inscribed "kallisti" into a big wedding celebration being held among the Greek gods and goddesses up on Mount Olympus. The inscription means "for the prettiest one," and party-goer goddesses Hera, Athena and Aphrodite all vied for the apple. Ill-fated Paris, Prince of Troy, was enlisted to choose the prettiest of the three. Bad plan. Girls will be girls and in this competition each goddess offered Paris a prize (it's called bribery now) if he would choose her. Boys will be boys and when Aphrodite offered Paris the most beautiful woman in the world, he quickly

awarded Aphrodite the golden apple. Trouble was, the most beautiful woman in the world was already married to the most powerful man in the world. There's more to the story, and there's a lot to be learned about leadership, ethics, group loyalty, and building horses out of wood throughout Homer's epic tale, too, but we'll wait for the movie to come out.

We're talking only about Eris here, because we're making a point that has less to do with ancient Greek history and everything to do with modern managers and leaders becoming exceptionally good. Back in Greece, circa 600 b.c., they would call exceptionally good leaders, heroes, especially if they did wonders with the kind of Hate Groups we're focusing on here. So, regarding Eris, or Strife, or Discordia, she made some trouble for the Greeks, and she could well be the mascot for modern Hate Groups, because her nature is to enjoy making trouble. And in this instance she tried extra hard because she felt snubbed by not being invited to that big Mt. Olympus wedding.

There are some lessons for us to learn from this story about action-reaction to the Hate Group. It is only normal to take it personally when the Hate Group attacks us. However, we shouldn't get too upset. Like Eris, some of the Hate Group simply enjoys making trouble because they like to be noticed or get tremendous pleasure from watching the commotion. This component of the Hate Group attacks everyone, so don't assume you have just been singled out for abuse. If you are now under attack, it is just your turn on the target. On the other hand, some of the Hate Group enjoys making trouble because you have snubbed or hurt them in some way. If they are attacking you because of this, you probably deserve it!

The dualistic nature of troublemakers

While Eris certainly does a lot of bad, the Greeks believed she also could do a lot of good. It was said that Eris could even stir up the shiftless to toil. Did the Greeks understand group dynamics or what? It is amazing what people can accomplish when they are dissatisfied with what they have, angry with critics who don't believe in their abilities, or frustrated with the way others are doing things. Perhaps discord has inspired some of our greatest triumphs.

A leader accomplishes very little by hating the Hate Group. On the contrary, there is a lot to gain by learning to love them, or (if that's beyond your abilities at the moment) at least remaining neutral. It is a very basic Sunday School lesson—love those who hate you. What we have observed in our studies of Hate Groups functioning in all kinds of businesses and industry is that when the Hate Group tries to hurt others, they often end up helping them reach their goals.

It has worked this way throughout history and against all basic logic. Consider the classic story of the Fall of Adam and Eve. Satan came to the Garden of Eden to create strife between man and God by tempting Adam and Eve to partake of the forbidden fruit. Satan succeeded in getting Adam and Eve to partake, but by doing so empowered Adam and Eve to become the mother and father of all mankind. Of course the disobedient act introduced many difficulties into the lives of Adam and Eve, but as we have already pointed out, strife and discord are not all bad. In the world of management, the Hate Group can make us look remarkably capable and strong when we know how to handle their attacks. The Hate Group can infuse a tremendous amount of energy into the business when we know how to correctly channel it. The Hate Group can become some of our strongest supporters when we are presented with just the right opportunity to turn them around and know the right way to do it.

Edison and Tesla: A series of unfortunate events

Today we take electricity for granted, but in the late 19th century there was still a battle raging over what sort of electricity we would be using in our homes and businesses. In one corner, Thomas Edison championed direct current (DC), the type of electricity we now get from batteries. In the other corner, Nikola Tesla challenged Edison with alternating current (AC), the type of electricity we now get from our wall outlets. Edison and Tesla were more than rivals.

They despised each other, but the story didn't start out that way.

Tesla came from a little village in what is now Croatia. He studied engineering in Austria. He tremendously admired Edison and his inventions. Upon seeing a demonstration of how Edison generated DC electricity, he immediately started searching for ways to improve upon Edison's ideas. This is typical Love Group behavior. Tesla's studies led him to develop important theories regarding the most efficient generation and use of AC electricity.

After immigrating to America, Tesla was eager to meet Edison so he could share his ideas about electricity. Edison agreed to meet with Tesla. At the meeting, Tesla shared all of his plans and ideas, but Edison wasn't impressed. Disappointed, but still hopeful, Tesla offered to improve the efficiency of Edison's electric generator by 25%. Edison accepted and promised Tesla $50,000 if he could deliver on his offer. Tesla worked from 10:30 am to 5 am the next morning, day after day, and week after week until he solved the problem. Edison, however, broke his promise and did not pay Tesla the $50,000 reward, calling the original offer just an "American joke." Bad decision on the part of Edison, who was never much of a comic. On that day, Tesla became a one-man Hate Group. From that day forward he vowed to never work for Edison again, and dedicated his most productive years as an engineer to finding ways to flip the "off switch" for DC electricity. Edison never thought in terms of Love Group and Hate Group, but he was about to learn a very important lesson.

If you hate the Hate Group, hold on to your hat

Edison was a tenacious worker. In his words, "genius is 1% inspiration and 99% perspiration." On the other hand, Tesla was a genius, plain and simple, and that is why the world runs on AC electricity today. After parting with Edison, Tesla redoubled his efforts. Tesla's ideas for generating and distributing electricity made Edison's work look rough, unsophisticated and amateurish. Tesla's AC could be carried safely and efficiently over long distances with thin and manage-

Thomas Edison

Thomas A. Edison (left) the great American inventor and Nikola Tesla (right). Edison paid a high price for hating the Hate Group, which ironically, he had himself created.

able networks of wire. Edison's DC required thick and clumsy spider webs of wire to maintain enough electrical power and reduce the chances for starting fires.

While Tesla improved his designs and gained funding from George Westinghouse, Edison ramped up his anti-Tesla propaganda machine. In a series of PR stunts, an Edison employee highlighted the killing power of AC electricity by "Westinghousing" stray cats, stray dogs, and even a circus elephant, inviting the press to such events. The coup de grace, however, was to have a murderer executed in the first electric chair using AC electricity to show what AC can do to a human. A newspaper of the day reported that the execution was an awful spectacle, in which the murderer had to be electrocuted twice and actually started burning.

After Edison mounted his grisly negative public relations campaign, nothing was going to stop Tesla from defeating Edison. Tesla bid against Edison for the contract to light the Chicago Exposition, Tesla and Westinghouse agreed to light the Exposition for just half of what Edison was asking. Edison lost the bid and was humiliated by Tesla's follow-up event. To show the public that AC current was safe if it was handled intelligently, Tesla donned heavy cork-soled shoes and used himself as an alternating-current conductor to light an incandescent bulb, amazing Expo visitors as he demonstrated the safety of AC electricity. After Tesla's extraordinary demonstration, Edison lost the war over who would light the world.

The high cost of hate

Edison admitted later in life that he knew that AC electricity was superior all the time. So why didn't he admit it and jump on Tesla's bandwagon when he had the chance? Some people struggle to explain Edison's behavior, but for anyone who has spent much time around managers behaving like Edison the answer is simple enough. For Edison, the only ideas with merit were his ideas. His leadership style was "my way or the highway." Perhaps he was emotionally, egotistically, and financially unable to accept the fact that Tesla had a better idea. What a shame. Fortunes were lost. Reputations were stained. The cost of hate is very high.

There is one final postscript to the story. Not many people know that Edison had an opportunity to be the first American to ever win the Nobel Prize. On November 6, 1915 the New York Times reported that the Swedish Government had decided to award the Nobel Prize for Physics jointly to Thomas A. Edison and Nikola Tesla, but Edison withdrew his name because he refused to share an award with Tesla. Consequently, the work of Edison and Tesla to light the world went unrewarded, at least in that prestigious way, and that year's prize went to William Henry Bragg and William Lawrence Bragg of the United Kingdom "for their services in the analysis of crystal structure by the means of X-rays."

Chapter THIRTY-FOUR

USE THE CRITICAL EYE

The Eye was rimmed with fire, but was itself glazed, yellow as a cat's, watchful and intent, and the black slit of its pupil opened on a pit, a window into nothing.

J.R.R. Tolkien

Some people have a gift for seeing faults and potential trouble everywhere they look. They have been born with what is called the "critical eye." They notice things in five minutes that others won't see in a lifetime. They get an adrenaline rush from being the "first to find" the flaw or problem. As they use that eye to peruse their surroundings, they are not necessarily trying to stir up trouble. They like to think that they are just being helpful.

We once had a colleague who was blessed with such an eye for spotting what was wrong with everything. On a regular basis he would draw us aside and brief us about all the things we were doing wrong in our classes. He based his analysis and warnings on snippets and opinions developed from what he had learned from students or other professors. Once he even took the time to diagram

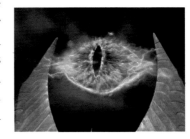

all the ways and underlying reasons one student thought we were "weird." While we were grateful for the effort, we have to admit that we never looked at that diagram. We already know we are weird. Our family members, in-laws, small neighborhood children and close friends have already pointed out all the identifying marks of our weirdness and we celebrate our condition; we wouldn't have it any other way. However, we still listened patiently to our colleague. As one might imagine, it was terribly painful, but ultimately we saw the good in it and his keen observations made us better teachers and people.

A while back we were presenting a seminar to the employees of a large company when we met a man there who is known among his associates in the workplace to have that critical eye. We had reached the climax of our presentation, which we modestly felt was the greatest presentation since Lincoln's Gettysburg address (or possibly that unforgettable two-hour speech delivered by Edward Everett that preceded Lincoln's). We revealed there in the meeting a carefully reasoned concept for a sales program that would undoubtedly increase that company's sales by twenty percent. When we finally concluded, all the employees stood up and cheered. All except one, Dan. The next day, Dan sent us a single sheet of paper containing a couple of phrases set in large type. It was obvious that this employee didn't buy into all the flair and celebration of the previous meeting. We will never forget the simple message on that paper.

All is good. All is well.

Now we have to work like hell.

Dan possessed the critical eye. He was able to cut through all the hype and promotion and made a simple observation that was fundamentally correct, when we sat down and did a little more analysis. Somehow, with all our graphs and charts and columns of numbers and statistics we had overlooked a salient point, one which Dan had somehow spotted from out there in the audience. We didn't have the manpower at the company to execute the plan as we had presented it. The sales plan was fundamentally correct, but everyone in the company would have to work 80 hours per week to make it happen. Dan's critical eye saved everybody from embarrassment. In every company there is an employee who possesses a special gift or talent that few of us understand. The critical eye can be described as a tenacious skeptical point of view. Employees who have developed this gift have a rare ability to see things that others rarely notice or even think about. They can see what's broken or missing in a plan, not just what parts of the plan work or will potentially work.

When the critical eye focuses its unflinching gaze on you, it is genuinely difficult not to react defensively. That's just being normal. Nobody likes to be told his carefully crafted idea has a weak spot (or in some cases that his whole project simply stinks). The attack on a manager's cherished plan by a critical eye can be relentless. It can cause even the most strong and capable leader to collapse in a pathetic heap, like J.R.R. Tolkien describes Frodo Baggins struggling to reach Mount Doom as he battles the influence of the Great Eye. The searing force of the Great Eye burns its image into his brain. He fights to be free of it, but he is enslaved by it until he destroys the ring that gives the eye its power. So it is with any of us when the critical eye turns its gaze in our direction. We want to run, but we can't. It sees all and all we can do, aside from picking up a serious drinking or drug habit, is to get its image out of our brain by addressing the concerns brought into focus by the person who has that critical eye and repair the faults. Just like Frodo, we must destroy whatever gives the critical eye its power: our own errors, which we just don't always see (and sometimes, which we see, but ignore because of our own egos). Recognize the critical eye for what it is: another tool in the arsenal of a well-functioning organization. Respect it. Cherish it. Make it work for your own good!

Over the years we have noticed many leaders appear rattled, ill-at-ease, and discombobulated when confronted by the critical eyes appraising the way they run their organizations and their plans for company growth. Right when the boss is launching a new program in all of its glory, that one employee with the critical eye turns his or her gaze towards the initiative and "tsst," all the passion of the initiative dries up like a drop of water on a hot frying pan. It's almost uncanny how, when a new program is being launched after months of calculations, brilliant thinking and astute planning, the critical eye is the first to see its limitations and kill the fun.

Before we discuss how managers should deal with the critical eye in one's own organization, we must acknowledge that we understand the blistering pain and intense suffering managers feel in the presence of the critical eye. It burns and stings. We know. In such circumstances, as the critical eye, speaking from way back in the folding chairs, points out those pesky little details that are critical, but which have somehow been ignored in the development of the big plan, it is not uncommon for a manager to experience the following symptoms:

- The mouth dries up and it is hard to talk because of the white chalky material building up around the mouth, lips and tongue.

- The face turns red and the manager-victim starts sweating uncontrollably. Every employee now thinks the manager is helpless, trapped in a corner like the proverbial rat in a trap.

- Some leaders figuratively start melting like the wicked witch in the Wizard of Oz. They stand there listening to their cherished plan being dissected with information they didn't think was germane to the subject, and now give new meaning to the term, "empty suit."

That's a tough situation, and managing people with a critical eye out there on the assembly line or in the mail room or over behind the accounting file cabinets can be demoralizing but it really doesn't have to be. Unfortunately, most leaders do one of two things when exposed to the searing heat of the critical eye: they either make tracks or make war. We don't believe either approach works very well. First, fleeing to get away from the critical eye may seem like a good idea, but a half mile down the freeway the leader is going to run low on second wind and realize that sooner or later he or she is going to have to go back to the company parking lot to get their car anyway. A more subtle way of relieving oneself of the fiery pain of its stare is done by not inviting the gifted employee, i.e. the one who has the gift of the critical eye, to an important meeting. That should show the Great Eye who's in charge here, right? On the other hand, we could simply get the "buy in" of a few key employees. We think you know who we are talking about; companies often have quite a surplus of them. Such tactics, however, only serve as temporary band-aids.

Other managers deal with the critical eye quite differently. They prefer to draw a line, stand their ground and make war. Like the knights of old, shielded by heavy armor and wielding the sword of authority they try to protect themselves from the fiery penetrating sparks and slay the critical eye. They verbally attack the negative views and endeavor to humiliate the employee with the critical eye. Alas for righteous war in the Conference Room, such tactics, while perceived as heroic by this type of manager, only create another Hate Group employee. This one, knowing full well that his or her comments were accurate, now sits in the shadows recruiting employees to the dark side and waiting for the right time to fight back. For example, when something goes wrong and top management is around to watch. Then, the critical eye gone wrong will shine a blazing light out of the shadows to expose the weaknesses and limitations of management's ideas, policies or programs. We often hear, "don't shoot the messenger," but in essence that is what we do when we make war on the critical eye (assuming, of course, that the employees with critical eyes in this discussion know what they're talking about, and because of our management blinders we always have to make that assumption). It's human nature for a leader to attempt to discredit and demoralize the bearer of bad news. After all, better that they are humiliated than us, right?

Regardless of how much it hurts, we must not shy away from the critical eye's blistering gaze. While many leaders view the critical eye

"On your resume you say you possess a 'critical eye.'"

© BYU Academic Publishing

as God's eleventh plague on mankind, or at least on those of us who aspire to wear suits and ties to work every day, in actuality it is an essential part of the creative process in every mature organization. That may sound like we are surrendering to the loudest negative voice in the company, but that's the wrong way to look at the critical eye phenomenon. It provides us with the balance we need to push our organization's boundaries of discovery. It is important for leaders to be enthusiastic, optimistic, and focus on the positive side of the equation. All great leaders have these qualities, but they must also have the ability to thoughtfully consider more than the positive elements in their ideas, policies and programs. Plus-One leaders also stretch themselves to consider their weaknesses and limitations, regardless of how they are exposed or who points out those weaknesses. Be a great leader, on whatever level you are in the organization. Train yourself to keep ego in check. Admit that sometimes even your best plan needs polish on the dull spot you have unconsciously concealed under your thumb (metaphorically speaking, of course). Appreciate the sudden and sometimes uncomfortable wisdom of your organization's critical eye. And then, to repeat ourselves, relax and use it for your own good!

Attempts to work with the critical eye may be awkward at first, but with time and practice it becomes easier—we guarantee it! We feel the best way to deal with the critical eye is to use the ABC process that public relations firms often suggest to clients when dealing with a crisis. The letters ABC stands for

Acknowledge,
Become part of the solution,
Change or Continue to Communicate.

Used in combination, these activities often will create a very special Love Group employee—one who has the critical eye. A Love Group employee with a critical eye is ten times better than a Hate Group member with a critical eye. Light side energy, to borrow again from Star Wars, is much easier to manage than dark side energy. Given a choice, we choose the light.

Acknowledging the helpfulness and penetrating vision of the critical eye is the smartest thing a leader can do.When someone picks apart your idea, program, or new policy, regardless of how minute the issue is relative to the overall program, thank and then adequately acknowledge the critical eye for their unique insight. Such acknowledgement makes the Great Eye feel valued. After all, we grow as an organization by not focusing on what has worked best in the past but by finding different ways to become truly remarkable for the stretch ahead. Thus the first step in dealing with the critical eye is to make sincere comments like, "Thank you for bringing the issue to our attention, it is something we have thought about in the past, but frankly need to spend more time on," or one might say "That is a unique insight that we haven't addressed yet. Perhaps we can talk together about that after this meeting if you have the time."

After acknowledging the eye, becoming part of the solution requires us to open ourselves up to the possibilities of another way to get things done. We must engage in real discovery, that is, take the skeptical comment of the critical eye and catapult the idea out in the open for employee brainstorming. To be part of the solution, we only need to allow our employees to push back the boundaries of current thinking to find new ways or new procedures for being a truly remarkable organization. When we become part of the solution, employees see us as courageously embracing new ideas; being a 360 degree leader; and showing full commitment to righting any wrong. For the feeling to last, however, we must change, right the wrong, or at the very least continue to communicate how we are planning for change. We have seen successful crisis management campaigns go wrong when the client talks the talk but simply won't walk the walk. This is a huge mistake. When the critical eye turns our way, we can't just talk our way out of the situation.

It is a magical transformation when leaders stop making tracks or making war in response to the critical eye. They ooze with confidence and employees enthusiastically get behind such leaders. Comments like, "Can anyone else see how we might overcome these issues" or "What other issues related to this problem should we consider to make sure this plan succeeds" start both leaders and followers down an exciting and winning path. Be on the lookout for employees with the critical eye. Don't be surprised by it. Be entertained and energized by it.

Chapter THIRTY-FIVE

BOOMERANG EFFECT

"Mr. President, I believe that enemies should be destroyed." To which Lincoln replied, "I agree with you sir, and the best way to destroy an enemy is to make him a friend."

Abraham Lincoln

It's not uncommon for the resident 500 pound gorilla in your organization's Hate Group to sling something unwelcome at you when you least expect it. Of course, this happens when you are most vulnerable and when the Hate Group believes it can cause you the most damage. Otherwise, why should they do it? Leaders, perhaps acting from deep in their reptilian brains, frequently and instinctively react in just the wrong way to questions from the floor like: "Why do we have these useless meetings?" or "Why do we need to participate in these stupid programs?" They come back at the askers with what can be best described as "brute force." Brute force responses are statements such as "because I say

so" or "because it is required by the company." These "react" responses rely on the leader leveraging his or her position of top-down authority. Bad idea. Such tactics only add fuel to the fire and amplify the destructive Hate Group feelings inside the firm. Fortunately, there are leaders out there who have gone through this refining fire in their organization and discovered a better way to respond to the Hate Group than confronting or even avoiding them. It's called the Boomerang Effect.

Let the boomerang fly back home

The Boomerang Effect is a tactic that is used when someone throws a negative comment or potentially embarrassing question at you. Think of that incoming statement from the Hate Group as a primitive airborne missile heading right at you. If you were a kangaroo—or a slow-thinking, quick-to-anger leader—you would be leaping off the stage, literally or figuratively, but you are a quick-thinking manager who thoughtfully underlined this whole chapter as you read it. Your responsibility now, as that missile comes at you, is to deftly return the negative comment, complaint, or difficult issue right back at them. Hence the term: Boomerang Effect. While it's easily defined, this tactic can be difficult to execute. In short, perfect execution of the boomerang tactic requires a leader to come into the meeting with (1) the correct mindset and (2) the correct skills. Let's begin by understanding the right mindset.

Having the correct mindset to effectively use the Boomerang Effect requires a good understanding of the principles of the ancient unarmed martial defense system called Judo. Author Carl B. Becker writes in *The Martial Arts Reader,* "Thus the principle of Judo, from the beginning, is not one of aggression, but of flowing with things." The word "Judo" means "gentle way." Judo's practitioners, whether among friends in a brightly lit training gym or in an back-alley brawl are supposed to act and react with minds filled with respect for their opponents, always beginning with courtesy and ending with courtesy. In Judo, one must learn to compete and prevail without contention, winning without overkill.

Judo skills focus on moving with the flow of the opponent's force, not against it, and never losing one's balance. (Let the opponents lose *their* balance, instead.) The Judo master must be "motion at rest," ready and capable at any moment to "give way," rather than using brute force to overcome an opponent no matter how big and tough they might appear.

The small and mighty

The Japanese national sport of Sumo reveres the lessons of Judo. The simple goal of Sumo is to get your opponent to touch outside the ring first. With such a goal, one would think that the sport would be dominated by the biggest and heaviest wrestlers. True, the real giants of this sport win more competitions than they lose. However, size alone can't explain the phenomenon of Chiyonofuji, The Wolf, who is one of the most loved Grand Champions in the history of the sport. He is significantly smaller than most of his Sumo opponents. In fact, he is so dwarfed by some of his competition that he looks like he shouldn't even be in the same ring. Yet, during one period in his remarkable career, he amassed 53 consecutive victories against Sumo's top-tier wrestlers. Even though he was very strong, he didn't win all those matches with brute force. He was smart. He was fast. He knew the only way he could win against much heavier opposition would be to use the massive weight and moving energy of his opponents to his advantage. Obviously, his version of the Boomerang Effect worked well for him in the Sumo ring.

Translating the Judo mindset into executing the Boomerang Effect means:

1. Courtesy first! Adopt a gentle way, not one of aggression.

    Never respond defensively or negatively to Hate Group comments, no matter what kind of attacks come your way. Responding defensively to employee comments compounds the difficulty of the situation. Being calm in adversity creates a powerful leader who will appear invulnerable to insult and innuendo.

2. Flow. Give way a little and don't push back.

    Learn to play along, as explained in earlier sections, and go with the flow of the situation. When we play along our personal defenses rarely show. Confidence abounds and we have the opportunity to neutralize and sometimes "win over" our adversaries before they even realize they are joining us.

3. Do not rely on your own strength to win the battle, but use the energy, either negative or positive, of others to your advantage.

    Plus-One leaders are self-confident, yet they rarely rely on their own expertise to deal with Hate Group criticism. They find multiple ways to keep their balance while the negative energy of the Hate Group swirls around them. They never stand alone because they know how to tap into and use the energy of those who surround them.

There are a variety of ways to execute the Boomerang Effect. Below are two key approaches for dealing with criticism, complaints or issues voiced by Hate Group members:

1. Ask other employees, especially some from your Love Group, to answer or explain the criticism that is directed at you.

    Employees from your Love Group will always defend you better than you could on your own. Furthermore, when employees respond to negative comments it reinforces the notion that other employees–not just you–see the positive side of the issue. Hence, negative energy thrown at you by the Hate Group is turned into positive energy from the Love Group. Having your Love Group field negative concerns makes the Hate Group realize that their idea is in the minority. Nobody likes to be in the minority group.

2. Thank the Hate Group spokesperson for their comment, although the comment is negative and perhaps hurtful. Praise them for their attention and insight into a complex issue.

    In short, recognize that all negative comments may well have a glimmer of truth or contain some valid idea. A Plus-

One leader must learn how to mine the idea and overlook the negative attack. Do this by first thanking the person for bringing the idea to our attention and being so perceptive. Next, take the idea or issue and turn it into a positive discussion. You and the Hate Group member will lead the discussion. In doing this, you strike at the root cause of Hate Group criticism. They just want to be noticed, heard and admired. The fact that they have not been seriously listened to or that their talents have not been appreciated is generally the root cause of their criticism. Remember, many of the Hate Group were once in the Love Group.

Changing negative comments into positive insights is always a winner. Managers should do this more often. Become the kind of manager who is happy to deal with employees who show real passion, whether it's negative or positive, about their work. Don't settle for cold and indifferent employees who enjoy smooth sailing. Lukewarm employees have little commitment to their jobs and contribute very little to a company's long term success.

Turning hate to love

The ultimate achievement of the boomerang effect is turning the Hate Group into the Love Group. We call it the golden boomerang! Leaders tell us that some of their strongest supporters were once in the Hate Group. While it seems that no one is turned from hate to love very often, we have some ideas about how it happens. The mechanism may look something like this:

1. A person openly and passionately reveals their hate. In so doing, they put themselves on thin ice and make themselves vulnerable.

2. The leader recognizes the vulnerability and quickly extends a hand to help the person back onto solid land rather than allowing them to stomp their way into the frigid waters below.

3. The person realizes their folly and grabs the leader's hand. The person has been brought to the Love Group.

Be Brave and Turn Hate into Love

When someone puts themself on thin ice, reach out a helping hand.

We recall hearing a young woman sharing a very personal and special experience that happened to her while she was serving as a missionary. She was given the assignment to visit Church members who had stopped attending Church services. After visiting with one single mother and getting to know a little bit about her and her family, the missionary asked a pointed question. "So tell me how you are feeling about the Church. Will you share your testimony about the Church with me?" The woman appeared to be a bit dismayed by the question, but then answered, "Oh, I know what you want me to say . . . you want me to say all those things we are taught to say as children in our Sunday School lessons, but I don't know any of those things."

The missionary sat quietly for a moment and then explained, "I wouldn't want you to tell me anything that you do not know . . . just tell me what you do know!" The woman thought for a few moments and then responded, "I know there is a God and that He loves us." The missionary said that she also knew there is a God and that He loves us. She then added how she felt knowing God lives and loves us is a precious gift and how that knowledge could bless the lives of millions of people. She then welcomed the single mother and her children to attend the upcoming Church services, expressed the pleasure of getting to know her and her family better, offered a brief prayer, and left. Only days after the experience, the missionary was transferred to another area. It wasn't until years later that the missionary found out the single mother and her family had gone back to attending Church services, and she had become an important women's leader in her Church community. The missionary had extended a helping hand during a critical moment and brought a woman and her family back to Church not just as a follower, but as a leader.

We fell in love with this story because in similar situations we have seen most people act very differently. We are sure you are familiar with the process. Someone in the Hate Group speaks their mind and challenges your beliefs. You then turn the spotlight right back in the face of the nonbeliever and look for faults in their life. Easy reaction, bad reaction. We think, certainly, if they do not believe the same things we do, there must be something wrong with them. Such behavior, however, only serves to entrench the Hate Group even deeper in their cynicism towards you and the organization. Instead of extending a helping hand, we usually tip the Hate Group off into the frigid deep of the dark side. And from that cold darkness, the Hate Group continues to gather strength and do as much harm as possible to our cause. We have hurt them at a vulnerable moment and they will never forget it.

We prefer to follow the uplifting example of the young woman and single mother. When all of the pain, hurt, and bitterness come to the top, be great and reach out your hand. Save someone. You won't regret it. This wonderful young-woman missionary had charisma, or should we say "caressme." She put aside her own feelings to protect and appreciate the sensitive feelings of that single mother and her family, and then miracles happened. This is the essence of Plus-One leadership.

APPENDIX

PLUS-ONE TACTICS QUICK REFERENCE GUIDE

Red Tactics
Survive the Hate Group

#01 GET OUT THE GARBAGE	Identify the "mindfields" before you step on them. Draw out thoughts about what you want to do before you do it. We often play the games Top Ten Answers or Refute the Critics to gather up the negative "baggage" surrounding an idea or project. The tactic allows you to (1) identify Love, Hate and Swing Groups, (2) discover issues or concerns that could undermine the success of a project, and (3) help you avoid doing or saying things that will hinder your ability to effectively lead.
#02 BE LIKE COLUMBO	Be like Columbo, not Sherlock! Take off some of the pressure of leadership. There is nothing smarter than acting "country dumb." It has an uncanny way of off-balancing those opposed to you and your plan. Play down your personal expertise, which may not be on as high a level as you think. Don't present your ideas and/or thoughts as if they are some rare treasure. Learn what others know and have to say before sharing what you think.

#03

PAI MA PI
(AKA PAT THE
HORSE'S
BOTTOM)

Praise people at every opportunity. Give them a great name to live up to. Be specific in your praise. A simple "preciate cha" will not suffice.

When you show confidence in others, they will have confidence in themselves. They will want to raise their level of performance to meet your high expectations. Always treat people like they are giving you their best.

#04

PLAY IT,
DON'T SAY IT

Most people don't listen as carefully or follow instructions as well as you expect them to. When you really want to get a point across, invent a game to get the point across for you.

Games we use often have something to do with competition. Everyone likes to win and usually will put out extra effort to get a victory.

#05

MANAGERS
SEE IT
LIKE...
EMPLOYEES
SEE IT LIKE

People are a bundle of emotions. We like to think that we are logical and level-headed, but there is a preponderance of evidence that shows we are not. Don't let negative emotions spoil relationships and a positive working environment.

At the first sign of conflict create some distance from the conflict for everyone involved by saying, "Managers see it like," and then continue to explain how managers at the company would view the situation. Then ask, how do employees at the company view a situation like this?" Continue the "managers see it like ...employees see it like" conversation until the conflict is resolved or at least moving in a positive direction.

#06

PLAY ALONG
...MOVE
ALONG

Stop criticism, negativism and outrageous behavior dead in its tracks, simply by having the courage and self-confidence to play along.

By "play along" we mean smile and agree, then improvise with a bit of humor or ask a probing follow-up question. For example, if someone points an accusing finger your way and says, "You don't have the skills or experience to do this job," smile and say something like, "I've often thought that same thing. Let's discuss it after the meeting."

#07

EXPLORE

When criticism and negativism won't stop even after you've played along, take time to explore the negatives. Openly and fearlessly exploring the criticism will make it wither. Ignoring the comments or being defensive will just nourish the criticism.

If criticism won't stop, simply look around at your team and solicit the comments from others who may have the same type of criticisms. Have someone write the criticisms down, then solicit the thoughts of those who don't have the criticisms. Find out why. Draw out the positive perspective. Never fight these battles by yourself. Remember that you have a whole group of people who will fight these battles for you and with you. Positive peer pressure will squelch the negativism better than you could ever do on your own.

#08

USE THE CRITICAL EYE

Some people have the gift to see faults and potential trouble everywhere they look. They have been born with the critical eye. Our first response is to fight to be free of it, but we are enslaved by it until we destroy the things that give the eye its power.

When the critical eye turns its searing gaze in our direction it is a crisis. So we suggest crisis management to take off the pressure and receive some payoff from all the pain. Use the ABC process that public relations firms often suggest to clients when dealing with a crisis. ABC stands for Acknowledge, Become part of the solution, and Change or Continue to Communicate.

#09

BOOMERANG EFFECT

When that 500 pound gorilla in your Hate Group slings an unexpected missile your way, don't react with brute force responses that rely on your authority. Instead, send those missiles on a return trip using the "gentle way" of the Boomerang Effect.

To send the boomerang back to the thrower, think courtesy first! Adopt a gentle way, not one of aggression. Next, flow with things. Give way and don't aggressively push back. Finally, do not rely only on your own strength to win a battle, but use the

#09 (CONT.)

BOOMERANG EFFECT

energy, either negative or positive, of others to your advantage. There are a variety of ways to execute the Boomerang Effect. Below are two key approaches for dealing with criticism, complaints, or issues of Hate Group members:

1)   Ask other employees, especially some from your Love Group, to answer or explain the criticism that is directed at you.

2)   Thank the person for their comment(s), although the comment is negative and perhaps hurtful, and praise them for their attention and insights into a complex issue.

Yellow Tactics
Engage the Fence Sitters

#10

SURPRISE PILES

Help people recognize and remember truth by using an outrageous example. More times than not, we don't get an "Ah Ha" until we first get a "Ha Ha."

#11

STUMP THE MANAGER

When a new program or policy is being implemented, put yourself on the spot and have employees try to stump you about the details. They will learn the details fast and you will connect with the employees by making some mistakes. Give prizes like movie tickets to anyone who stumps you.

#12

THOUGHTS & FEELINGS

When you introduce new information to people, ask them to write down (1) a summary, (2) questions and (3) their thoughts and feelings. Then ask everyone to share what they've written until all of their comments are drawn out.

#13 TEAM DEBATE	When there is a controversial issue that people can't agree on, divide the employees into three groups. Have one group advocate one side of the issue, one group advocate the other side of the issue, and the third group act as judges. Perhaps even ask people from your Love Group to act as judges.
#14 LEAN & SMACK	Sometimes people need to be smacked. Set up a situation in which they reveal flawed attitudes and/or ideas. Then indirectly confront the misperceptions. A manager wanted employees to support a recognition program. To launch the idea, he showed a short film describing several exceptional companies at a team meeting. One clip showed a woman tearfully receiving an award for Employee of the Year. The manager saw detractors chuckling during the clip. So after the film was over, he mentioned that it was amazing that an award could be important enough to make someone cry. The detractors nodded in agreement and chipped in criticisms. The manager then stepped forward and said quietly, "but I want to let everyone in on a secret ...we are building more than a business here, we are building people...being able to build up their people is what makes that company great. And that's what I want for our company."

Green Tactics
Empower the Love Group

#15 PAINT THE TARGET & SHOW HOW TO HIT IT	The Love Group wants to please and they can get frustrated and annoyed when they don't know how to do it. Be very specific about desired outcomes, guidelines, expected level of work, and then let the employees alone. If you do this the right way there will be no need to look over shoulders or micromanage. Employees will "fill in the blanks" with creativity and energy!

#16

FIRST IN
LAST OUT
(FILO)

The Love Group wants to make a personal connection. Look for opportunities to make it easy for the Love Group to connect by being the first into team meetings and the last one to leave team meetings. Occasionally come in to work early and leave late to see who is around and talk. Bring some food. You get the idea!

#17

JUMP ON
THEIR
BANDWAGON

Employees in the Love Group want to solve problems and make things better for everyone. Try not to squelch the love because it is easy for managers to get defensive when employees make unsolicited suggestions. Look to the Love Group for vision and jump on their bandwagon.

#18

MAKE A
MINI-ME

Employees in the Love Group will help you fight tough battles. Learn to engage them when you are under attack or don't know what to do next. Don't worry about being upstaged. Have the courage to give them authority not just responsibility. Make them a hero. Make them a leader. Make them a Mini-Me.

#19

REWARD
BEFORE
THEY BEG
FOR REWARD

When the Love Group has to beg for help, recognition, a raise, or a promotion, no success or reward is big enough to compensate for the disappointment and bitterness that begging can create. To them begging means that their extraordinary efforts are underappreciated and overlooked. It makes them feel that their dedication and loyalty have been ignored. That's when they move to the dark side and start looking for another job.

All employees like unexpected rewards, but no one enjoys them more than the Love Group. Even simple rewards can be effective, particularly when it extends recognition beyond the workplace to friends and family.

INDEX